Y0-DKB-533

AMERICA, A HOUSE DIVIDED

The Social Conservative Movement: Pure Religion or Hypocrisy?

—∿—

Herschel Hill

PRESS

Copyright © 2006 by Herschel Hill

AMERICA, A HOUSE DIVIDED
by Herschel Hill

Printed in the United States of America

ISBN 1-60034-436-4

All rights reserved solely by the author. The author guarantees all contents are original and do not infringe upon the legal rights of any other person or work. No part of this book may be reproduced in any form without the permission of the author. The views expressed in this book are not necessarily those of the publisher.

Unless otherwise noted, all Scriptures are taken from the Holy Bible, New International Version, copyright © 1973, 1978, 1984 by the International Bible Society. Used by permission of Zondervan Publishing House. The "NIV" and "New International Version" trademarks are registered in the United States Patent and Trademark Office by International Bible Society.

www.xulonpress.com

CONTENTS

—ɯ—

ACKNOWLEDGMENTS

—ɯ—

This book is dedicated to my lovely wife and best friend, Aileen, who encouraged and supported me as I researched material used in this book, selected and studied pertinent Scripture passages, and penned the words written herein.

I also want to express my gratitude to the many journalists, editors, and news reporters who provided much of the material utilized in this book. I could not have accomplished this study without the factual information contained in numerous commentaries, editorials, and news reports published during the last four years.

Most of all, I am thankful for the Holy Spirit whose guidance and revelations enabled me to gain a greater understanding of the Scripture passages incorporated into this book. My prayer is that the results of my Bible study, as reflected in the pages herein, are true interpretations of the Bible passages utilized.

Jesus knew their thoughts and said to them, "Every Kingdom divided against itself will be ruined, and every city or household divided against itself will not stand."

—Matthew 12:25 NIV

CHAPTER 1

America in Year 2006

—m—

America is a house divided in year 2006; partisanship and bitter division characterize relations
between citizens of our country. What was essentially a
united nation fifty years ago has gradually evolved into a
polarized population. We are evenly divided politically,
with each side assuming inflexible positions on most of
the issues. Our country has always had two major political
parties, and we have certainly seen partisan division on
many issues in the past. However, we have always been
able to reach bipartisan agreements on a large number
of the issues, and both political parties seemed to seek
what was best for our country. Partisan debate about the
issues was usually civil, and that debate was beneficial
and healthy for our nation. Compromise and give-and-
take was the rule of the game in Washington until some

twenty-five years ago. That bipartisanship has vanished; the Republican and Democratic Parties take opposite sides on virtually all the issues in today's society, with both sides being unwilling to compromise.

This book explores the emergence of that bitter division in our nation and considers some of the sources of the polarization. It is difficult to pinpoint the exact time the trend started, and it is equally difficult to identify all the causes of the increased partisanship. Many factors are involved and related, but one area examined closely is the possible contribution of the Christian social conservative movement to the extreme partisanship that exists in America today. Has the social conservative movement contributed to the bitter division in our country, and if so, how has it come about? That is one of many questions we consider as we attempt to determine why our nation is so bitterly polarized.

Factors leading to the polarization of our citizens are discussed in the first few chapters of this book, together with the effects that division has had on our nation. Later chapters examine Biblical teaching pertaining to key moral and social issues relevant to today's society. We look closely at what the Bible has to say about those divisive issues our country is trying to deal with. Our goal is first to consider from a Biblical perspective some of the problems inherent in our society and then to suggest ways to eliminate much of the extreme partisanship gripping our country. I am convinced most of the rhetoric and finger-pointing originate in the extreme right and the extreme left fringes of our population.

Mainstream Americans, I believe, desire an end to the bickering and animosity we see throughout our society. However, if we are to end the extreme partisanship in our country, those folks in the middle must become keenly aware and knowledgeable of the issues, and they must become actively involved. In other words, they must vote those individuals with radical and inflexible views out of office, thereby taking back control of our country. That is a tall order considering the relatively low percentage of eligible voters who participate in our electoral process. It is thus imperative that a greater number of our citizens exercise their right to vote. The right to vote is one of the freedoms that men and women have fought and died for, and one that citizens of numerous other nations of the world do not enjoy.

America has experienced a rapidly growing social conservative movement over the last twenty years. That movement, which is religious in nature, was initiated by the so-called religious right, and their primary objective is to increase the role and influence of the Christian religion in our nation's policies and politics. The first major player in the social conservative movement was a group called the Moral Majority, headed by Jerry Falwell and other religious conservatives. That initial group was replaced gradually with a larger and broader political organization referred to today as the Christian Coalition, or religious right.

Growth of the social conservative movement has been fueled primarily by narrow and strongly-held beliefs concerning key moral issues such as abortion, euthanasia, homosexuality, and school prayer. Republican conservative politicians embraced social conservatives and incorporated their views and beliefs into the Republican Party agenda. At the same time, Christian social conservatives adopted the Republican Party's policies and views with regard to gun control, pro-business policies, anti-affirmative action, school voucher systems, tax policies, and other non-religious issues. Today, social conservatives are a sizable and integral part of the Republican Party, and the Christian Coalition, or religious right, has a tremendous influence on Republican Party policy. Social conservatives are an extremely committed and a very active constituency, hence they are major players in local, state, and national politics. The Republican Party of today is essentially defined and characterized by the social conservative movement.

No attempt is made in this book to either affirm or reject the religious and moral beliefs held by social conservatives. Our objective is not to question or contradict their basic views on such issues as abortion, euthanasia, and gay marriage. Instead, the emphasis in our study is on the possible negative impact the Christian conservative movement has had on our society because of the religious right's attempts to incorporate their particular beliefs and practices into our nation's laws and government policies. We look closely at the fundamentalism, intolerance, and narrow-mindedness inherent in the social conservative movement. The problem is not what social conservatives believe about various moral and social issues. For the most part, their views are consistent with those of many other Christians, as well as a lot of non-Christians. The problem is that they try to force everyone to adopt, and abide by, their beliefs and practices. That, I believe, has created much of the division and partisan strife prevalent in our country today.

Certainly not all conservative Christians have participated in, and supported, the social conservative movement. Many conservative Christians place a higher priority on issues that are not religious or moral in nature. They are more interested in, and involved in, non-religious social concerns, fiscal issues, foreign policy, and labor matters. For the most part, the social conservative movement has been driven by very conservative, or fundamentalist, Christians who place utmost emphasis on hot-button moral issues such as abortion and homosexuality. Their views on such issues are the result of their very narrow interpretation of the Bible, or Scripture, and they are intolerant of people with different beliefs.

This mixing of religion and politics, together with the inflexible and somewhat radical views of those on both ends of the religious and political spectrum, has yielded a bitterly divided country. Political campaigns, deliberations in Congress and our state legislatures, implementation and enforcement of our laws and regulations, and conduct of foreign policy have become increasingly more partisan and mean-spirited. The main concern for most politicians and their campaigns is to get reelected and to seize an advantage for their political party. They do not appear to be genuinely concerned about what may be best for our country. There are, of course, quite a few politicians who are deeply concerned about the partisan strife at all levels of our government and the overall health of our country, but their number seems to be dwindling.

Some of our citizens argue that America is better off as a result of the increasing influence of social conservatives, whereas others maintain that the social conservative movement has caused much of the division and antagonism in our nation. At first glance, one could conclude that an increase in Christian influence would be beneficial for our country. However, if that Christian influence is not achieved in a spirit of love and unity of purpose, it could be detrimental to our great nation. Perhaps that is why our founding fathers incorporated separation of church and state into our Constitution and Bill of Rights. They realized religion and politics don't always mix well. One of our goals in this book is to determine if the social conservative movement has indeed been beneficial for our country.

America is an extremely diverse nation, and it has always been somewhat divided because of differences in race, religion, and economic status. But that past division is nothing like what we see today. Today's extreme partisanship, developed to some extent as a result of the social conservative movement, has led to a rollback of much of the progress made by our country over the last seventy or so years in civil rights, labor relations, and consumer protection. Social conservatives, in partnership with so-called fiscal conservatives, have chipped away at our civil rights laws, reduced protection of workers and consumers, and increased the gap between the wealthy and the poor. Much of that rollback in the areas of civil rights and economic class distinction has evolved from the social conservative movement. And, at the same time, religious partisanship and strife increased dramatically.

The changes wrought by the social conservative movement are in evidence throughout our society.

The policies, laws, and practices emanating from the social conservative movement have influenced our political system, our school systems, our legal system, our welfare system, our health institutions, our business environment, our financial systems, our churches, and our foreign policies. Much of this influence on our society has been direct and obvious, whereas a large part of it has been indirect and more subtle. Perhaps the most troubling outcome of the social conservative movement in America is the antagonism, division, strife, and plain old mean-spiritedness in which our citizens relate to one another.

The Christian social conservative movement is supposedly grounded on moral and religious beliefs, so why has it created so many problems in our country? Social conservatives claim their views and actions are based on Biblical principles and Biblical teaching, and they cite Scripture to justify their stands on moral and social issues. A major goal of this book is thus to determine if the social conservative movement has pure religion as its foundation or if it is grounded in hypocrisy. Social conservatives cite the Bible, or Scriptures, as their guideline, so let us delve into the Bible to determine if their claim is true.

We examine applicable Scripture passages in both the Old Testament and the New Testament in this study. Scripture quotations are from the New International Version (NIV) of the Bible. The truth and authority of the quoted Bible passages are without question, but the views, conclusions, and comments included herein represent the author's interpretation and understanding of Scripture. You, the reader, most likely disagree with a number of the interpretations and views expressed by the author, but let us have an open mind as we attempt to interpret and apply Biblical truth to the critical issues facing our nation.

Other factors have certainly contributed to the dramatic increase in partisanship and division in America. The growing influence of big money in politics has yielded greedy and corrupt politicians, laws and regulations favoring special-interest groups, a legal system tilted toward big business and the wealthy, unfair tax policies, and huge budget deficits. Politicians, and their votes, are bought by big-money interests, so the average citizen in our country has virtually no say regarding the direction our nation is heading. In today's political environment, lobbyists for special-interest groups dictate, and sometimes even write, the laws and regulations passed by Congress and the state legislatures. The result is tax breaks, legal protection, biased laws and regulations, and obscene profits for the special-interest groups the lobbyists represent. Taxpayers like you and me foot the bill for this corruption at all levels of our government.

Another major factor is the enormous changes taking place in our nation's news media. Our federal government manipulates and controls by coercion our news services in order to get news reports and news commentaries that are favorable to their point of view and their policies. Unbiased reporting of the news is becoming quiet rare. Our radio, television, newspaper, and internet news services are becoming more and more just mouthpieces for the political interests with which they are aligned. A large number of our citizens listen only to those news outlets that tell them what they want to hear; they refuse to listen to any view other than their own. That is especially true for those people who get their news and commentaries from the talk shows, tele-

AMERICA, A HOUSE DIVIDED

vision networks, internet news outlets, and newspapers aligned with the social conservative movement.

Our nation's education system is also changing as a result of the social conservative movement. We see an increasing number of private and church-sponsored Christian schools and universities that teach their particular brand of religion. As such, many of them are intolerant of any religious beliefs other than their own. Those private Christian schools and universities tend to be more fundamentalist in nature, hence they are strongly committed to their religious causes and are more apt to support the social conservative movement. What is inherently a good thing, Christian schools, turns out to be a detriment to our nation's health because of the partisanship it fosters. Rather than the Christian love and unity we associate with religion, we see bitter division and animosity.

Our country was extremely polarized well before our invasion of Iraq. We all remember the down-and-dirty presidential campaign in 2000, which was decided by a Supreme Court decision. Al Gore won the overall popular vote, and the outcome was in doubt for weeks awaiting the final vote recount in Florida. The Supreme

Court stepped in and halted all recounts, thus handing the presidency to George Bush. The Supreme Court essentially appointed George Bush as president by a narrow five to four decision, after having overruled the State Supreme Court of Florida. That debacle just amplified the mean-spirited partisanship that existed in our nation.

The Bush administration's later decision to unilaterally invade Iraq, together with all the problems that decision created, was the straw that broke the camel's back. Animosity and polarization have increased dramatically in our country as the casualties have mounted in Iraq and the war's cost keeps spiraling up. What was estimated by the Bush team to be a quick and easy war with a duration measured in weeks or months, and with a cost of no more than $60 billion, has stretched into some three years with no end in sight. The direct cost of the war in Iraq is now approaching $400 billion, with the indirect costs being much higher than that. A subsequent chapter in this book addresses the conduct of the war in Iraq and some of the divisive issues associated with it.

Our country is split right down the middle, with both sides taking inflexible positions. The 2000 presidential election was decided by a razor-thin margin in Florida and the Supreme Court intervention. The 2004 presidential race was almost as close, with the slim margin in Ohio favoring George Bush being the deciding factor. Both houses in Congress are almost evenly divided, although the Republican Party does enjoy small majorities in both houses. And, most controversial issues brought before the Supreme Court are decided by five to four decisions. As a result, battles in the Senate over confirmation of Supreme Court appointees are very partisan and extremely fierce. Hardly any bipartisan issues are left in America today. For the most part, we see Republicans fighting against Democrats on virtually every issue of any significance.

America faces difficult problems arising from the division and bitterness within our citizenship. Our nation's problems are very complex and hard to understand, but the root causes of those problems are even more complex and more difficult to comprehend. We attempt in this book to shed some light on the factors leading to our bitterly divided country, particularly those factors evolving from the social conservative movement. Also considered are possible ways to reduce the partisanship and division in our nation.

CHAPTER 2

A Bitterly Divided Country

—⁊⁊⁊—

Our nation has always been divided to some extent. We pride ourselves in being a democracy, and by nature a democracy incorporates and encourages differences of opinion among its citizens. These varying opinions are expressed in America by means of political parties and elections in which voters select their government representatives and decide crucial issues. In addition, our nation's Constitution and Bill of Rights provide basic protection for minority groups of our citizens. That precludes the majority from forcing their will on the minority even though they may have voting control at various levels of government.

The intent of our founding fathers, I believe, was to establish a government that is best for our country as a whole and one which meets the needs of all our citizens. They were careful not to favor one class of people over another or to promote one religion over other religions.

Thus, we have separation of church and state in our Constitution and Bill of Rights. Freedom of religion, or freedom from religion, is one of the fundamental freedoms for which men and women have fought and died for throughout the history of our great nation. Separation of church and state has served America well for over two centuries, but it seems now that many social conservatives are endeavoring to tear that wall down. They want to incorporate their particular religious beliefs into our laws and government policies. Essentially, the religious right wants to legislate its own brand of morality.

Our nation appears to be drifting more and more toward a culture of fundamentalism, both in religion and in politics. Segments of our population have developed very strong and very narrow views with regard to specific issues within our society, including those dealing with religion. For many of those issues, such as that of abortion, you will find sincere and committed people with opposing beliefs. A large number of those on both sides of such issues have quite radical views. They will not tolerate any view other than their own, and their political support of a party or a candidate is dependent almost solely on that party or that candidate's position on the issue they are most concerned about. Those are single-issue voters.

Those radicals tend to be activists, and they are extremely outspoken in their support of, or opposition to, specific issues. They consider almost any action to further their cause to be justified, legal or not. We thus see torched abortion clinics, harassments of both businesses and individuals, and riots of various kinds. A more subtle and a more prevalent form of such activism is that of spreading outright falsehoods or innuendos about either the issues or those people on opposing sides of the issues. Negative politics, or mud-slinging, has become a popular and very potent tool for winning elections, and manipulation or misrepresentation of factual data has become routine in establishing and justifying government policies. The internet is used extensively by radical groups to disseminate information and falsehoods that further their particular causes.

We normally associate fundamentalism with religion, but with the advent of the social conservative movement, we now see more fundamentalism in politics. Because the Christian Coalition, or religious right, is so closely aligned with the Republican Party, it is difficult to differentiate between religion and politics. Issues that once were in the realm of religion are now in the political realm as well, and other issues that were previously deemed political in nature have since been embraced by Christian social conservatives. Religious beliefs are thus becoming a significant part of political debate and government policy. This is true at local, state, and national levels, but it is particularly disturbing to see religious beliefs become such an integral part of federal government policy.

Racial and ethnic issues and concerns have historically been the most significant divider of our country. First, of course, was the terrible and inhumane incidence of slavery in our nation's early history. The North and South fought the long and bloody Civil War, primarily over the issue of slavery. That was followed by lengthy struggles to attain voting rights and equal representation for minorities, who were for the most part African Americans. We all remember the violence, strife, rioting, and overall hard feelings that accompanied the long struggle to integrate our public schools, businesses, restaurants, workplaces, and public facilities. More recently, we have observed proponents of the ongoing civil rights movement seeking to provide minority segments of our citizenship with equal opportunities for education, better housing, fair job and career opportunities, access to adequate health care, and access to legal representation. Tremendous gains have been made in all these civil rights areas, but more must be done.

Racial tension and strife had gradually diminished until about twenty years ago, or at about the same time the social conservative movement was initiated in earnest. Although civil rights laws and regulations remain in place, federal funding and federal oversight have been reduced to the point that civil rights laws and regulations are not adequately enforced. The conservative Republican Party, with enthusiastic support of the religious right, has gained control of our national government and many of our state governments. The inherent bias within the Republican Party against social programs such as Social Security, Medicare, Medicaid, affirmative action, equal opportunity, government housing projects, welfare, and minimum wage control have resulted in a rollback of many of the civil rights gains of the previous fifty years or so. We have therefore witnessed a dramatic increase in the bitterness and division due to racial and ethnic issues, and minority segments of our nation, especially African Americans, have turned to the Democratic Party.

The racial and ethnic division in America has rapidly evolved into a broader and more general division, that of economic class. It has turned into a struggle between the have's and the have-not's, or between the wealthy and the poor. What once was predominately an African American problem has since encompassed poor Mexican Americans and poor Caucasians as well. Many of them live in slum neighborhoods, go to inferior schools, have inferior roads and utility services, work on low-paying jobs, have limited access to health care, exist on essentially perpetual welfare, seldom vote, and have virtually no access to legal representation.

For the most part, these poor people are the forgotten masses in America; they are under the radar. The average citizen in our nation is not even aware that such poverty and hopelessness exist in America, and for those who are aware of it, they do not seem to care. In budget decisions at both the federal and state levels, benefits and funds for our poorer-class citizens are the first ones to be cut. Tax cuts and tax breaks are granted to the wealthy and to big business at the expense of the poor working class. Our elected representatives give lip service to the problem, but they do very little to help those people rise above their current station in life. Needless to say, such poverty and adverse living conditions breed discontent, bitterness, hopelessness, violence, and crime. Our jails and prisons are full of people that came from such a background. Much of the violence and crime in our country stems from the neglect of those pockets of poverty in all of our major cities and in many rural areas. The solution to the problem is not to build more jails and prisons. Instead, we must take action to reduce poverty and alleviate the adverse living conditions in those areas.

Closely related to the division our country experiences between economic classes is the division we see between big business and labor, or between employers and employees. Fifty years ago, employers were loyal to their employees, and employees were, in turn, loyal to their employers. Many workers spent their entire careers with the same company, never worrying about job security. Employers provided steady employment, fair wages, and reasonable benefits for their workers, and most large companies offered generous retirement plans to their employees. The result was contented and productive workers. Business and labor got along well for the most part, even with the occasional strikes by union workers.

The business environment we see today is vastly different from that of fifty years ago. Loyalty has virtually disappeared on both sides, with the average worker having numerous employers over the course of his or her career. Greed and corruption have replaced loyalty and trust in the workplace. Mergers, widespread transfer of jobs overseas, mass layoffs, obscene salaries to management, elimination of retirement plans for workers, reduction in medical benefits for employees and retirees, and factory automation have changed the business landscape drastically. Most companies place utmost emphasis on the bottom line, with minimal concern for what is best for their employees. The result is worker dissatisfaction and anxiety, tension and bitterness between management and employees, and high turnover of employees. Productivity and quality suffer in this type of workplace environment.

Another significant source of division in our nation is the diverse views held by our citizens regarding the environment. Stark differences of opinion exist with regard to how we use, or abuse, our land, water, air, and natural resources. Business interests such as mining companies, timber companies, oil companies, petrochemical companies, manufacturing companies, and land developers are motivated by corporate profits rather than by environmental considerations. Many of them have no qualms about polluting our lakes, rivers, and streams if it enhances their bottom line. The effects of their pollution on marine life are of no consequence to them, and they do not worry about possible harmful effects to human beings who may drink the polluted water.

In a like manner, these same corporations spew out pollutants into the atmosphere, thus poisoning the air we breathe. Such industrial air pollution, together with the pollution generated by the trucks and automobiles we drive, account for a significant part of the global warming effect the world has experienced in the last few decades. And, the problem is getting worse, not better. Laws and regulations are in place to control much of this pollution, but they are not enforced by an administration favoring big business interests over the health and welfare of our citizens. Our current Republican administration in Washington has rescinded or crippled many of our environmental laws and regulations, and funding has been slashed to the agencies responsible for enforcing the regulations. Hence, the polluting industries are essentially left to regulate themselves; we have the fox guarding the henhouse.

Much of our public land is open to mining operations, timber harvest, and oil exploration, so wildlife sanctuaries are being altered or destroyed. At the same time, the natural beauty and wonder of our parks and publicly held land are adversely affected. Greedy land developers have created problems around our cities regarding flooding, mud slides, inadequate fire control, and inadequate traffic control. A majority of the mining companies, timber companies, oil companies, and land developers have sacrificed the public good at the altar of corporate profits.

A large number of people in America are greatly concerned about environmental issues. Some of them cling to extreme, or radical, views and are quite active in their opposition to the corporate identities who pollute our land, air, and water and degrade our natural and pristine lands. They are just as vocal against the politicians and government agencies who condone and support the corporations responsible for polluting the environment. The result is bitter division and animosity in our nation because of this general corporate disregard of the environment. Some corporations, politicians, and government agencies do care greatly about the environment, and they are striving diligently to resolve environmental issues in such a way that our quality of life will be maintained or improved. However, in our present culture of greed and corruption, these good Samaritans are swimming upstream; their task is extremely difficult.

Numerous other special-interest groups in our country have issues near and dear to them. One such issue is that of gun control. Many gun enthusiasts consider their right to bear arms and own any weapon of their choosing to be their number one priority. They are very outspoken and very intolerant of any opposing view. On the other side are those citizens who believe just as strongly that guns are responsible for much of our violence and crime, and they do not believe people have the right to own all kinds of guns. Again, the end result is extreme bitterness and division in our country over the issue of gun control. There are many similar controversial issues in our society which result in division amongst our citizens, some at the local level and some at the national level.

The Christian conservative movement spawned a partisanship in America that has spread throughout our society. It is a division that has its roots in religion, or religious beliefs, but it has rippled across almost every aspect of American life today. The foremost issue in the social conservative movement is that of abortion, but the religious right also focuses on issues such as homosexuality, gay marriage, euthanasia, prayer in public schools, the teaching of Biblical creation in public schools, including God in our pledge of allegiance, and displaying the Ten Commandments in public buildings. The intense partisanship developing out of the social conservative movement can be traced to inherent fundamentalism within the religious right, or the Christian Coalition.

The religious right considers the division in America over religious beliefs to be a good versus evil struggle, with them being on the side of good. Social conservatives refuse to accept any religious views other than their own, and they strive to incorporate their particular beliefs into the laws of our land. For example, the religious right seeks to teach the Biblical account of creation, which is a fundamental Christian tenet, along with evolution, an established scientific theory, in our public schools' science classes.

Such teaching of creationism, which some refer to as intelligent design, is a religious belief based on the Biblical account of creation in the Book of Genesis, and it does not belong in a science or biology class in a public school. It is the opinion of this writer, a devout Christian who believes strongly the Genesis account of creation, that science and the Bible are not contradictory. The Bible addresses the "why" and "who" of creation, whereas science focuses on the "when" and "how." Although I do not understand just how it can be, I believe science and the Bible, God's Word, are fully compatible. I believe the Word of God, the Bible, and the works of God, scientific facts, are consistent. Humankind does not yet possess the knowledge to ascertain one hundred percent correlation between the Bible and valid scientific findings, but I am certain that it does exist. School boards across America are experiencing bitter struggles over this one issue, and it is the subject of political debate at both the state level and the national level.

The battle over abortion rights is being waged at every level of our society. It seems unbelievable, but one's belief about abortion has become a litmus test for nominees to the Supreme Court of our land. The mean-spiritedness and malicious activism associated with the debate about abortion rights are shocking for a civilized nation like America. Abortion doctors have been murdered, abortion clinics have been destroyed, abortion clinic patients have been verbally and physically harassed, and businesses and careers have been destroyed, all in the name of religion. Those supporting legal abortions are almost as avid in their belief as those opposed, so there is no apparent end to the battle, regardless of what our Supreme Court may rule in future decisions.

The sad fact about the whole abortion rights issue is that both sides really want the same thing. Those on both sides of the issue want to reduce the number of abortions in our country and around the world. The difference is how the two sides propose to achieve that goal. The religious right, the Pro-Lifers, want to make abortion illegal, and thereby force pregnant women to deliver their babies regardless of the circumstances involved. However, most Pro-Lifers show little concern for the welfare of the babies before and after they are born. Those favoring legal abortions, the Pro-Choice adherents, want to keep abortion legal, but most of them do seek viable alternatives to abortion. They are also more likely to be involved and active in seeking ways to reduce unwanted pregnancies. One way of doing that is to provide better sex education to young people, including making contraceptives available to young girls who insist on being sexually active. On the other hand, most Pro-Lifers insist on abstinence-only sex education classes in our public schools, and they strongly oppose distribution of contraceptives to our young people.

I do not have the solution to the abortion problem, but I believe it must incorporate more rounded sex education for our youth, practical measures to reduce the number of unwanted pregnancies, better prenatal care for expectant young women, viable alternatives to abortion, proper medical care and support for those young women who do choose abortion, and adequate medical care for babies who are the product of unwanted pregnancies. Simply making abortion legal or illegal will not solve the fundamental problem of too many young women having unwanted pregnancies.

Christian social conservatives want to incorporate their religious beliefs into our nation's laws, but that is in opposition to our country's tradition of separation of church and state. Our nation's largest Protestant denomination was at the forefront for many decades in the battle to maintain separation of church and state, as provided in our Constitution and Bill of Rights. That early battle was primarily over the issue of funding parochial schools with tax money. That same Protestant denomination is now leading the fight to tear down the wall of separation between church and state. Did God and His will change over the last forty or so years? No, I do not believe so. Did God's Word, the Bible, change during that time period? Again, the answer is no. Did that Protestant denomination change? The answer must be yes; that denomination is now a religious fundamentalist body with very narrow and strongly-held beliefs.

The religious right has taken strong and inflexible stands on other issues as well. They oppose legalized gay marriage and any form of homosexuality, they oppose euthanasia for any reason, they support state-sponsored prayer in public schools, and they insist on placing the Ten Commandments in public buildings. Social conservatives strive to have all their beliefs on those issues incorporated into our laws and government policy. We see strong opposition on each of those issues, and the result is sharp division among our citizens. The religious right is also heavily involved in other controversial issues that are inherently political in nature rather than religious. Those political issues are discussed in the following chapter of this book.

CHAPTER 3

Extremely Partisan Politics

—〰—

Our nation has always had a democratic two-party form of government, with division of power between the Executive Branch, Legislative Branch, and Judicial Branch. Ours is a system of checks and balances, and our Constitution and Bill of Rights ensure that the ruling majority does not trample on the rights of the minority. That government structure has served our nation well for over two hundred years, even during the times when one political party had control of all three branches of government. Such a two-party system of government is partisan by nature, but that partisanship has been limited and healthy for our country. A majority of our past political leaders were committed to doing what was best for our country. For the most part, they placed the overall welfare of our nation over what was advantageous at the time for their political party. I consider that to be true statesmanship.

The political landscape in America has changed drastically, however, in the last twenty-five years. We now see extreme partisanship at both the federal level and the state level of our government. Why is that? I do not have a simple and straightforward answer for that question, but I believe we can identify several factors that have contributed to our increasingly more partisan political system. Some of those factors are religious in nature, whereas others are not. It is quite difficult to differentiate between religious factors and those that are purely political in nature because of the close ties developed between the religious right and the Republican Party.

Social conservatives are very passionate about their religious beliefs, and that passion has carried over to nonreligious issues incorporated into Republican Party policy and adopted by the religious right. In addition, the Republican Party has embraced many of the religious views of social conservatives with equal fervor. The extreme religious partisanship of the religious right has thus been integrated into the entire Republican Party agenda, both religious and nonreligious. Our country experiences the same bitter division over supposedly nonreligious issues such as gun control and protection of the environment as we do over religious issues such as abortion rights and gay marriage.

The culture of fundamentalism inherent in the social conservative movement has penetrated the political realm as well, especially the Republican Party. Staunch Republican conservatives are passionate about key issues, they are inflexible in their stands on those issues, they will not accept any opposing views, they work diligently to further their causes, they are united in their efforts, and they will do almost anything to discredit or destroy those opposing them on the issues. The Republican Party, together with the religious right, is extremely well organized, and they have mastered the art of negative campaigning. Opposing political candidates have been discredited and defeated by spreading falsehoods and innuendos about them by means of television blitzes and internet news outlets. The Republican Party and the religious right consider political battles to be warfare between good and evil, and they equate their particular positions on the issues to the side of good.

In the political process, they attempt to demonize the opposition.

Republicans and social conservatives have a history of personal attacks and smear tactics against opposition candidates. They look at liberalism in much the same light that communism was considered during the cold war; they deem all liberals to be evil. Decorated war veterans have been called liars and fakes, other severely maimed and decorated war veterans have been called cowards, many of our honest and upright citizens have been labeled as soft on crime, and worthy opponents have been called unpatriotic simply because they disagreed on foreign policy issues. It is disgraceful that elections can be won using such unscrupulous tactics, but that has been the norm in recent political campaigns. It is a mere reflection, I believe, of the bitter political division in our country.

Closely related to this fundamentalism is the ideology championed by the Republican Party leadership. Many Republican policies and decisions are based either on personal agendas or on strongly-biased viewpoints on key issues. The Republican Party leadership chooses to ignore factual information that may dictate a direction different from the one they have chosen, and they reject credible analyses or evidence showing the negative impact of continuing on their chosen path. It is difficult to differentiate between fundamentalism and ideology in the Republican Party because religion and politics are so closely entwined. Their narrow-minded view and strict adherence to the Republican Party agenda are detrimental to our country. The Republican Party leadership, and especially the current Bush administration, does not want to be confused by facts. The Bush administration refuses to admit their mistakes and failures, and they stubbornly stick to their failed ideological agenda. We see this in both foreign policies and domestic issues. Needless to say, such stubborn adherence to flawed and failed policies leads to bitter division in our nation.

Conservative Republicans, with the always faithful support of the religious right, press for laws and policies favoring wealthy people and large corporations. Generous tax breaks, numerous tax loopholes, and handouts to key industries cost our government, and thus taxpayers like you and me, billions of dollars each year. Middle-class Americans and our poorer citizens thus have to shoulder an unfair and unequal share of the overall tax burden. One such tax avoidance policy allows big businesses to set up offshore corporations in order to shield a large portion of the overall corporations' profits from taxation. That one tax avoidance scheme costs our nation's treasury billions of dollars each year and provides those corporations with unfair cost advantages over similar corporations who do not have such tax shields.

Another example of conservative Republican policy favoring large corporations is that of the Medicare prescription drug program initiated in early-2006. That program was supposed to provide senior adults with significant savings on their prescription drugs. Instead, it turned out to be a very complex program, structured by lobbyists for insurance companies and pharmaceutical companies to give their clients huge windfall profits while yielding minimal savings for only a small percentage of our senior adults on Medicare. That sham prescription drug program also allowed pharmaceutical companies to continue charging obscene prices to the citizens of our country, as opposed to the much lower prices charged in Canada and Europe for identical drugs. That is especially brutal and unfair to our senior citizens on fixed incomes. The Medicare prescription drug fiasco has caused much distress and bitterness within our senior adult population.

Republican policy favoritism toward rich people and big business is evident throughout our society. The Bush administration's huge tax cuts are heavily tilted toward wealthy people and large corporations, budget cuts have been directed primarily at social programs, environmental regulations have been relaxed for the benefit of big business, tort reform legislation has made it more difficult for consumers to sue corporations, revisions to bankruptcy laws favor banks and other financial institutions, and the federal government has passed much of the costs of social programs down to the states. All those changes were made by a Republican Congress at the direction of the Bush administration. And, this is an administration and political party that claim to be "compassionate conservatives." Perhaps their definition of compassionate conservatism is different from that of most Americans.

The Bush administration has pushed two rounds of tax cuts through a compliant Republican Congress. Included was a one-time tax rebate for many taxpayers, which was received with great enthusiasm by most recipients. However, the significantly larger long-term tax reduction is skewed heavily toward the wealthy and large corporations. A mind-boggling fifty percent of the total tax reductions are to the richest one percent of our citizens, and about eighty percent of the tax cuts go to the richest twenty percent. That is in an economic environment wherein wealth in our society is already being transferred steadily from the lower and middle classes to the richest ten percent of our population. The Bush tax cut plan accelerates that shift in our nation's wealth from the poor to the wealthy, thus widening the disgraceful wealth and income gap between the wealthy and the poor.

In addition to the reduction in income tax rates for all taxpayers, the Bush tax cuts include reductions in inheritance taxes and dividends taxes. Those are taxes paid primarily by wealthy individuals, so the tax savings benefit primarily the wealthiest segment of our population. All the biased Bush tax cuts are on top of the unfair tax savings already enjoyed by wealthy individuals and large corporations who use a variety of tax shelters and take advantage of tax loopholes set up to benefit special-interest groups. To add insult to injury, the Bush tax cuts were sold to Americans in the name of fairness and equality in our tax system.

Most discussions on income tax cuts ignore another significant tax that all wage earners pay, the payroll tax, consisting of Medicare and Social Security deductions. Because a majority of the payroll taxes are not paid on income above a fixed threshold, lower-paid wage earners have to pay a larger percentage of their total income for the payroll tax. The percentage of total income paid in payroll taxes is therefore small for those individuals making very high incomes. Additionally, payroll taxes are not paid on any income from sources such as interest on savings, capital gains, and stock dividends. That has virtually no impact on low-income citizens because they do not have such income, but high-income individuals are spared paying payroll taxes on vast amounts of their income. The resulting total tax burden, income taxes plus payroll taxes, is a very unfair and unequal tax load for the lower and middle classes of our citizens.

The Republican Party, including social conservatives, is pressing for elimination of the present income tax. They want to replace it with either a national sales tax or a flat income tax, wherein all taxpayers pay the same percentage of income tax. That change to a national sales or a flat income tax is trumpeted as being more fair and equal to all taxpayers. Analysis quickly reveals, however, that either the flat tax or the national sales tax would reduce the overall tax burden on our wealthiest citizens but increase it on all low-income and middle-income Americans, assuming no change in the total amount of taxes collected. Such a scheme does not seem very fair or equal to me, but I do not claim to be a compassionate conservative so what do I know.

Most states have three primary sources of income to fund our public schools, namely a sales tax, a local property tax, and a state income tax. A few states, such as Republican-controlled Texas, do not have a state income tax. Lower-income wage earners in Texas thus pay a much larger percentage of their total income in taxes than do Texas' wealthier citizens. Such a tax system is inherently unfair, and the incorporation of a state income tax would tend to equalize the tax burden for all citizens. However, a state income tax in Texas is highly unlikely in the foreseeable future because of the dominance of the Republican Party and social conservatives in state politics.

A good example of the prevailing climate in the Bush administration and Republican Congress regarding taxes and tax collection is a mandate to the Internal Revenue Service (IRS). The IRS was instructed by Republicans to crack down on fraud involving the Earned Income Tax Credit, which is available only to the low-income working poor. On the other hand, the Republican Congress discouraged the IRS from spending much effort going after fraud by high-income taxpayers. In essence, the IRS was told to utilize their limited resources to collect small amounts of money from poor people while allowing wealthy individuals to underpay their taxes by very large amounts. That is indicative of an administration taking care of their well-heeled friends and contributors but trying to punish those poor people more likely to be Democrats.

A majority of Americans realize taxes are a necessity if our government is to provide the services we need and want. And, I believe most of our citizens are willing to pay their fair share in taxes. The problem is that some greedy individuals and large corporations want to shirk their responsibilities to pay taxes and thus pass that burden on to someone else. In our present culture of greed and corruption, it seems to me that many of our wealthier citizens and businesses belong to that group which wants to pass their tax responsibilities on to someone else, and they strive to change our tax laws to benefit themselves. All of this strife over taxes is the source of much division in our country.

The Republican Party, with the ever loyal support of the religious right, seems to be against virtually any program that benefits poor people. That is true at both the federal level and the state level. The Children's Health Insurance Program (CHIP) is under-funded, student loans are being cut back and interest rates increased, funding is inadequate for Child Protective Services, eligibility requirements for Medicaid are being tightened and funding reduced, funding for public schools is being reduced, veterans benefits are being cut, requirements for welfare are being tightened and funding cut, and funding for elder care and handicap care are being reduced. Those actions seem strange for an administration and Congress that preaches compassionate conservatism. Perhaps we see a little hypocrisy in the Republican Party and the Bush administration.

In their fervor to enrich the wealthy, large corporations, and well-heeled special-interest groups, the Republican Party has rolled back many of the laws and regulations designed to protect the environment. Corporate profits are more sacred to them than clean air, pure water, and unpolluted land for our citizens. Timber companies, oil companies, mining companies, land developers, petrochemical plants, and manufacturing companies operate with limited oversight and control by our federal government. The result is polluted air and water, hazardous waste in our land, destruction of wildlife sanctuaries, and damage to our pristine parks and land. The Bush administration does not even admit that the environment is adversely affected . Government reports relating to global warming, pollution, and other environmental issues are essentially censored by them. The Bush team omits portions that are critical of administration environmental policies and sometimes fudges the numbers to support their biased views on the issues. What we see is cherry-picking of environmental data by the Bush administration to establish and support flawed environmental regulations and policies. Obviously, such disregard for the environment causes bitterness and division with those activists who are committed to protecting the environment.

Our Congress and state legislatures are partisan by design in our two-party system of government. Debate about the issues is healthy as long as fairness and civility are maintained. Unfortunately, fairness and civility have virtually vanished in both wings of Congress, especially in the House of Representatives, and in a majority of our state legislatures. Extreme partisanship has been the norm in Congress throughout the Bush administration. And, that is with a president who campaigned as a "uniter" rather than a "divider" in year 2000. The majority Republican Party has tried to run roughshod over the minority Democratic Party in Congress. Democrats are shut out from the decision making process regarding the legislative agenda, and they are not kept informed about the contents of many controversial bills. Democrats are forced into voting on the bills, quite often with very little time to review the contents of the legislation.

The Republican leadership makes most legislative decisions behind closed doors, often with administration officials present, and deals are made without Democratic input. Numerous bills are brought to the House floor for a vote with provisions never discussed in full committee or debated by the House. In addition, the House leadership regularly uses threats and outright bribery to coerce hesitant Republican representatives to vote in agreement with the leadership position, sometimes holding the vote open for hours in order to garner the necessary votes. That particular maneuver is the source of much of the pork barrel spending we hear so much about, now referred to as earmarks, wherein funding for pet projects back in the representatives' home districts are incorporated into the bills.

One such bill was the Medicare prescription drug plan passed in 2005. Lobbyists for large pharmaceutical companies and insurance companies were heavily involved in crafting the bill, which just happened to include huge subsidies for their clients. The Bush administration assured Congress the Medicare prescription drug plan would cost no more than $400 billion over ten years, which was the maximum amount Congress agreed to, when in reality administration officials knew the costs would be much higher. Thomas Scully, a Bush political appointee, instructed Medicare officials not to divulge the true cost estimates of the plan to Congress. Even with the falsified lower cost estimate, the House leadership had to break House rules and hold the vote open for three hours before they could strong-arm the required number of House Republicans into supporting the bill. That sort of partisan skulduggery is commonplace in Congress, especially in the House of Representatives.

Another source of bitter contention in both Congress and our state legislatures is the issue of "family values" and morality. The Republican Party, and particularly the Christian Coalition, claims the high road on that issue, insisting that our society is headed toward moral bankruptcy because of the liberal influence. They maintain that their beliefs on religious issues such as abortion rights, homosexuality, gay marriage, prayer in public schools, and the teaching of creationism versus evolution in public schools are based on the Bible and its teachings. Their claim may or may not be true, but they choose to ignore clear Biblical teachings on numerous other moral issues in our society.

The Bible condemns the greed and corruption that is running rampant in America, and it tells us in no uncertain terms that we should care for, and have compassion on, the poor and powerless in our society. That surely includes the elderly in nursing homes, our severely handicapped citizens, uninsured children, abused women and children, people living in abject poverty, our homeless population, the mentally ill, and other similar downtrodden segments of our population. Funding for programs to meet the needs of those helpless, and sometimes hopeless, citizens is the first to come under the budget-cutting axe of the compassionate conservative and family values Republican Congress. Such heartless treatment of our most vulnerable citizens has the full support and blessing of our current Republican administration. Other moral issues such as marriage infidelity, high divorce rates, the high incidence of teenage pregnancies, denial of adequate legal representation for the poor, and unequal educational opportunities for the underprivileged must be addressed, but the Republican Party gives only lip service to those important issues.

All of these religious and moral issues are discussed in greater detail in later chapters of this book, including what the Bible has to say about some of the issues.

CHAPTER 4

The War in Iraq

—⟋⟍⟍—

The September 11, 2001, terrorist attack on our great nation halted temporarily the escalating polarization and division in America. People in this country always seem to come together during such a disaster, especially if it comes from an outside source. The surprise attacks by Al Qaeda terrorists on the twin towers and the Pentagon cost almost three thousand American citizens' lives, wrought billions of dollars in property damage, put our financial systems into a state of chaos, brought to a halt commercial airline travel, and disrupted our whole way of life. But through it all, our citizens displayed resilience and a resolve to fight back at Osama bin Ladin and his terrorists.

Our country seemed to put aside animosity and division to rally around President Bush as he led us in driving Al Qaeda and the fanatical Taliban regime out of Afghanistan. We were on the verge, I believe, of defeating the Al Qaeda terrorist network and capturing their leader, Osama bin Ladin. America had the encouragement and support of our allies around the world, and there was little sympathy for the radical Islam faction responsible for the attack on America. Then, something strange happened. The Bush administration diverted its attention away from Osama bin Ladin and his terrorists and began to focus on Saddam Hussein and Iraq.

Americans have strong differences of opinion about the conduct of the war in Iraq and the reasons we initiated that conflict. It is primarily a partisan disagreement, with a majority of Republicans and the religious right favoring the Bush administration's actions and most Democrats being opposed to the unilateral invasion of Iraq. The bitter division and animosity thus returned to our nation with a vengeance. I read and heard a multitude of news accounts and commentaries, both pro and con, about our invasion of Iraq and the conduct of that war. I find it very difficult to sort out the facts and determine what information is credible and what is not. I struggled to gain an understanding of why and how the decision was made by the Bush team to invade Iraq, carefully considering personal statements made by key individuals on both sides of the issue. I studied numerous media reports and commentaries, realizing many of them came from biased sources, and I diligently tried to account for those biases. I observed very closely comments and news reports from individuals and media outlets I considered credible, reputable, and unbiased.

There are some areas, I am sure, in which the information utilized in this study is not completely factual, and some of the data derived from news reports and commentaries may be somewhat misleading. I am confident, however, that my overall assessment and comments regarding the ongoing war in Iraq, as well as the events leading to it, are valid. It is imperative that we focus on the big picture, not getting bogged down in the details, as we try to analyze the conduct of the war in Iraq. I fully recognize, however, the extreme partisanship associated with any discussion of the war in Iraq and the events leading to it.

President Bush and his inner circle of advisors seemed to have their wrath aimed at Saddam Hussein and Iraq from the time of the 9/11 terrorist attack on our country.

What was the reason for that vendetta against Iraq? A number of people believe it was personal in nature because of the criticism directed at President Bush's father, the first President Bush, for not taking Saddam Hussein out during the Gulf War some ten years earlier. Others say it was revenge against Saddam Hussein and Iraq stemming from the failed plot to assassinate the first President Bush. Another possible reason put forth by the pundits is the vast amounts of oil reserves held by Iraq, oil that the Bush team would dearly love to gain control of. Still others point to the Bush administration's unpopular domestic agenda prior to September 11, 2001, and the tremendous boost in President Bush's approval rating after the invasion of Afghanistan. His political advisors, primarily Karl Rove, knew President Bush's approval rating, and thus his chances for reelection, depended on our country being at war; his questionable domestic agenda would not occupy center stage during wartime. I believe all of those factors were in play as the Bush team steered America into an ill-advised unilateral invasion of Iraq.

There is widespread disagreement and debate regarding the events leading to America's invasion of

Iraq and the justification for doing so. A critical lack of credible intelligence data was certainly one of the leading factors in the flawed justification to invade Iraq. There is much speculation, and significant evidence to suggest, that the Bush administration rejected valid intelligence data that was contradictory to their claims about Iraq, while at the same time fabricating and promoting inaccurate intelligence data to support their claims. In other words, the Bush team cherry-picked and manipulated intelligence data to justify their predetermined plan to invade Iraq and remove Saddam Hussein from power. Subsequent findings and events in Iraq, together with statements from key people within the intelligence community, indicate that such cherry-picking and manipulation of intelligence data did indeed take place. If true, America was deceived into invading a sovereign nation without sufficient justification.

The Bush team maintained that Saddam Hussein posed an eminent threat to our country. They painted the picture of a fanatical tyrant who possessed weapons of mass destruction (WMDs), including biological weapons, chemical weapons, and possibly nuclear warheads, together with the capability to deliver them.

We all remember seeing on television and in newspapers sketches and descriptions of mobile biological and chemical weapons laboratories that Iraq supposedly possessed. We were also told that Iraq had modified their legal short-range missiles to obtain illegal long-range missiles capable of delivering biological, chemical, or nuclear payloads. The Bush administration informed us that Saddam Hussein was acquiring material from which nuclear weapons could be developed and that he had an ongoing program to develop such nuclear weapons. All those claims about WMDs in Iraq were subsequently proven to be false, as reported in the 9/11 Commission Report.

A second reason given by President Bush and his inner circle for invading Iraq was the close ties between Al Qaeda terrorists and Saddam Hussein. That also proved to be a false claim. No connection was found, either in participation by Iraqi citizens in Al Qaeda terrorist activities or in financial support of the Al Qaeda terrorist network by Iraq. In actuality, a majority of the nineteen terrorists who attacked America on September 11, 2001, were from Saudi Arabia, one of our allies, and a significant amount of Al Qaeda's financial support has

been traced to Saudi Arabia. Using the Bush administration's criteria to support the invasion of Iraq, perhaps
we invaded the wrong country. In addition, Saddam
Hussein's brutal regime in Iraq was a secular one rather
than a religious one, whereas the Al Qaeda terrorist
network is led by, and comprised of, religious fanatics.
That is the primary reason Saddam Hussein had nothing
to do with Al Qaeda. In fact, Christians in Iraq suffered
minimal persecution under Saddam Hussein's reign; he
did not feel threatened by them.

Not only did the Bush administration mislead our
country into believing the unilateral invasion of Iraq
was justified, they also tried to win the support of our
allies through the United Nations (UN). Except for
Great Britain, most of our major allies rejected the
Bush team's ill-conceived argument; hence, we had to
go it alone in Iraq without the United Nations' blessing.
America has furnished a great majority of the troops
and practically all the funding for execution of the Iraq
war. In the process, the Bush team has alienated some
of our staunchest allies and tarnished America's image
around the globe. Mild dislike of America has turned
into intense hatred in some parts of the world, particu-

larly in Muslim countries. Our country is looked upon in many parts of the world as a rich, arrogant, and powerful bully who covets the oil produced in the Middle East and attempts to force its democratic way of life and Christian religion on the rest of the world. That sort of attitude toward America breeds terrorists, as evidenced by a sharp increase in terrorism in all parts of the world, especially in and around Afghanistan and Iraq.

How has the war in Iraq affected Osama bin Ladin's terrorist network? If Osama bin Ladin had been given a choice about what our country could do to best aid his terrorist cause, he most likely would have answered, "Invade Iraq." The Bush team has given Osama bin Ladin the best terrorist recruiting tool he could hope for. America has invaded an Arab country with little if any provocation, we have alienated many of our allies, tens of thousands of innocent Iraqi civilians have been killed, we are attempting to gain control of Iraq's vast oil reserves, we are occupying an Arab country in an Arab part of the world, Arab prisoners have been abused and tortured, we have destroyed or taken over thousands of innocent Iraqis' homes, and we are attempting to force our brand of democracy on the Arab world. Iraq was a country devoid of terrorism, except for that inflicted upon his own people by Saddam Hussein, but it has now become the breeding ground and center of activity for terrorism. That includes the Iraqi insurgency and the Al Qaeda terrorist network, which are becoming more and more entwined. And, the number of insurgents and terrorists in Iraq is steadily increasing, not decreasing as the Bush administration would have us believe. The roadside bombs, car bombs, and suicide bombers are becoming more sophisticated, better coordinated, more potent, and more frequent.

The war in Iraq has been waged for three years, with no end in sight. Reconstruction progress is extremely slow, the insurgency and terrorist activities are increasing, Iraq is having to import oil to meet the country's needs, political unrest is growing despite democratic elections, a religious government rather than a secular one seems eminent, fraud and corruption are running rampant in Iraq, the cost of the war keeps escalating, closer ties between Iraq and a fundamentalist Islam Iran are being developed, and Iraqi citizens want American troops out of their country. All those developments are contrary to what the Bush administration projected when they were pressing for authorization to invade Iraq. President Bush and his inner circle ignored words of caution and warnings from people with years of experience dealing with Middle East Arab affairs. Many individuals who have in-depth knowledge and understanding of Arab culture and the Islam religion predicted the kinds of problems that our military has experienced in Iraq.

The Bush team expected a quick and easy victory over a regime they considered to be weak militarily. They claimed their "shock and awe" bombardment of Iraq, especially Baghdad, would convince Saddam Hussein's troops to throw down their arms. And, they told us the Iraqi people would welcome our troops as liberators. Defense Secretary Donald Rumsfeld predicted the war would last weeks or months, at most two years. He also estimated the cost of the war and postwar reconstruction to be about $60 billion, with the optimistic assumption that Iraqi oil sales revenue would pay for a majority of those costs. In actuality, the direct cost of the war and associated reconstruction effort in Iraq is approaching $400 billion and still climbing. We do not know if those were actual expectations and projections from an honest but incompetent administration. Neither do we know if they were purposely misleading and deceptive claims from an administration bent on invading Iraq, regardless of contradictory world opinion and intelligence data suggesting a delay in such a hasty invasion. For either scenario, key people in President Bush's inner circle should be removed from their positions.

Another point of contention was the number of troops necessary for a successful invasion of Iraq. Some military leaders, both active and retired, pegged that number at about 200,000, but the Bush administration was unwilling to commit that many troops. Some military leaders lost their jobs because they voiced their honest opinions about the troop strength needed for such an undertaking. President Bush has told us repeatedly that the field generals will get the troops they ask for. That was his claim before the invasion of Iraq, and that has been his contention throughout the ongoing three-year war. What he does not tell us is that any field general asking for a troop level above what the administration is willing to commit is subject to dismissal from his position. What field general would go against the wishes of his Commander-in-Chief, knowing his military career was at stake? They simply go along to get along. Neither does President Bush let us know that Paul Bremer, the civilian administrator in Iraq from 2003 until 2004, repeatedly asked for additional troops to control the insurgency. All of his requests were ignored by the Bush team, so troop strength on the ground in Iraq was insufficient to contain looting of ammunition dumps and government buildings, and our military was unable to prevent infiltrators from coming into Iraq from neighboring countries.

It is quite obvious the Bush team did not plan for the strong and widespread insurgency that developed after our invasion of Iraq. Apparently, there was no contingency plan whatever in the event the Iraq invasion did not go as expected. It is almost unbelievable that the leaders of a world power like America could be so naive in planning for war against another nation. I have to believe our senior military officers had little input in the planning and preparation for the invasion of Iraq. Perhaps the civilian decision makers at the White House were so confident they were right about Iraq that they considered a contingency plan to be unnecessary. Or, perhaps the Bush team believed that development of a backup plan for Iraq would be perceived as a sign of weakness, an indication they could be wrong in their assessment of Iraq. Remember, those were actions of a President, and an administration, who refuse to acknowledge any error or wrongdoing.

Regardless of the reason for our military not having a contingency plan for Iraq, the war has been a disaster for our country. After a quick initial victory, wherein Baghdad was bombarded from the air and our troops marched victoriously the length of Iraq into Baghdad, Saddam Hussein was left essentially with a powerless military. He was a toothless tiger. Iraq provided very little organized resistance against America's powerful military machine. Many Iraqi citizens did indeed welcome our troops as liberators, and we all remember seeing the Iraqi people celebrating the demise of their ruthless dictator, Saddam Hussein. Our television sets were filled with the images of the Iraqi people toppling statues of their evil leader. I am sure the Bush administration was elated by the outcome of the initial invasion of Iraq, but their celebration was premature.

Saddam Hussein had hundreds of huge stockpiles of military weapons and equipment scattered throughout Iraq, and most of them were left unguarded during the weeks following the fall of Baghdad to our military. Additional soldiers should have been available to secure those weapons sites, but the Bush team had not planned on such a contingency, and the needed troops were not available. Needless to say, many Iraqis helped themselves to those vast stores of unguarded military arms and ammunition. That was the source of much of the weaponry and bomb making material that was to be used by insurgents to kill and maim American troops in the following three years. We have to ask, "Why was all that military equipment left unguarded for so long?" I do not believe the Bush administration has a satisfactory answer for that question.

Next, the highly questionable decision was made to disband Saddam Hussein's military. Surely, our military leaders in Iraq realized the need for strong security forces in postwar Iraq. Local police forces would be a necessity, and a national military presence would be required to maintain order during postwar reconstruction. The logical thing would be to utilize trained and seasoned Iraqi soldiers to meet those security needs, realizing that hard-line troops loyal to Saddam Hussein must be weeded out. The alternative was to train and equip raw recruits to staff local police forces and a national military, a task which would be time consuming and costly. Once again, naivety and incompetence triumphed over reason, and the remnants of Saddam Hussein's army were disbanded. However, serious effort to train and equip Iraqi security forces was delayed many months, allowing the Iraqi insurgency and imported Al Qaeda terrorists to become entrenched in Iraq. Such bungling of security in postwar Iraq is inexcusable, and those responsible in the Bush administration should be fired.

Surely the Bush team should have expected the rise of an insurgency in Iraq and an influx of Al Qaeda terrorists from surrounding countries. If they did, it was not evident, because very little was done to impede the increase in insurgency within and the flow of terrorist recruits from without. Additional troops should have been allocated to Iraq to control the insurgency and reduce the influx of terrorists until adequate Iraqi security forces could be trained and equipped. In addition to killing hundreds of American troops and thousands of Iraqis, insurgents and terrorists have kept oil production to a minimum, slowed reconstruction efforts to a crawl, crippled the fragile economy, and terrorized innocent civilians. All of that has turned many Iraqis against our country. They blame us for their problems and want our troops to leave their country. That is not what the Bush administration expected in postwar Iraq.

Another glaring problem with prewar planning and preparation was the unforgivable lack of protection for our soldiers. Troops were sent into battle with little or no personal body armor, and their vehicles had inadequate armor to protect against roadside bombs. Even today, three years into the war, all of our troops do not have sufficient body armor, and many of their armored vehicles are not protected as well as they could be. In fact, many families of our soldiers have purchased body armor for their loved ones, and soldiers in the field in Iraq scrounged scrap metal to re-enforce the armor on their vehicles. That lack of adequate armor has resulted in higher death rates and more serious injuries to our fighting men and women in Iraq. Perhaps additional tax breaks and tax subsidies for wealthy people and large corporations are more important to the Bush administration and Republican Congress than the safety of our military personnel in Iraq. Why are so few Americans concerned about the misplaced priorities of our nation's leaders? Our incompetent and uncaring Republican leaders should have to answer for their bad decisions and failed policies.

Who is doing the fighting and dying in Iraq, and who in our country is making the sacrifices necessary to pay for such a costly and bungled war effort? For those of us who can remember World War II, we know the fighting and dying in that conflict and the sacrifices for the overall war effort were shared by all segments of our population. Teachers, lawyers, factory workers, bankers, farmers, retailers, accountants, politicians, engineers, movie stars, sports stars, poor people, rich people, and others from all walks of life fought together and died together in the war against Germany, Japan, and Italy. That is certainly not the case for our war in Iraq. For the most part, our military is staffed by men and women from the working class, especially from rural areas and minority segments of our population. How many sons and daughters of the politicians and bureaucrats in Washington who committed our country to war do we see in Iraq? Not very many, I am sure. The Bush administration and their well-heeled supporters do not mind committing someone else's children and grandchildren to war as long as their own families do not have to go.

Other than the price paid by our military personnel and their families, what is the cost of the war in Iraq? What sacrifices have we had to make? What sacrifice have you made? Our lifestyles have not changed, we still drive our gas guzzling automobiles and SUVs, we do not have rationing of any goods, the wealthy people and corporations have their tax cuts, large companies and corporations enjoy their tax subsidies and tax breaks, energy conservation is something we do not want to hear about, mandatory military service is not required, and we do not have to pay the cost of the war in Iraq. Huge budget deficits are funding that war; obscene national debts are being passed on to our children and grandchildren. How can someone be truly patriotic and stand by while such unfairness and utter disregard of personal responsibility permeate our society? There is more to patriotism than supporting President Bush and his flawed policies in Iraq.

Phony patriotism is a trademark of the Bush administration, the Republican Party, and most social conservatives. They equate patriotism to supporting President

Bush and his decision to go to war in Iraq and to supporting our military in Iraq. If I support President Bush and his decision to wage war against Iraq, does that mean I am patriotic? On the other hand, if I do not support our president and his unilateral decision to go to war with Iraq, does that mean I am unpatriotic and do not support our men and women in the military? Sadly, many people today answer yes to both questions. That should not be so. We have been bombarded for three years with media reports and commentaries pertaining to support of President Bush and our military in the war with Iraq. A large number of our citizens believe strongly that the invasion of Iraq was unjustified and that the Bush administration has led our country down a dangerous path. Many others, however, support with equal passion our president and his decision to invade Iraq . Quite a few of this latter group also state unequivocally that those opposed to President Bush's decision are unpatriotic and imply strongly that they do not support our soldiers in Iraq .

We live in a country where freedom of speech is a constitutional right, yet those who speak out against President Bush and his decision to invade Iraq are castigated for their stand. That has been especially true for entertainers and sports stars. The issue of patriotism has personal implications for me. I am a veteran of the Korean conflict, although I was fortunate to miss out on combat duty. I love my country, I wore the uniform of our nation with pride, and I served to the best of my ability without questioning my assignments. Millions of other men and women have served in our military, and not a few of them gave their life to keep our great nation free. One of those freedoms is that of free speech, a right we must never give up.

I strongly support our men and women in the military in our war against Iraq. I sincerely believed, however, that our unilateral invasion of Iraq was not justified and that it would lead to many serious problems for our country and the world as a whole. Removal of Saddam Hussein and his brutal regime was certainly desirable at the time. The Iraqi people and the rest of the world are better off with him out of power, but the same could be said of other nations who have corrupt and evil dictators. Iraq posed a possible potential threat to the security of our nation, but not any more so than other rogue nations such as North Korea and Iran. And, the perceived threat from Iraq was not eminent. The Bush administration had ample time to work through the United Nations. The arrogant rhetoric and diplomatic blunders of the Bush team leading to the decision to go to war, together with the unilateral invasion of Iraq, alienated many of our friends around the world. Our nation's actions have thus created new enemies and motivated terrorists and would-be terrorists to commit acts of violence against our country and its interests. I share the belief of many others that our country is faced with much greater risks from terrorism as a result of our invasion of Iraq. That increased risk is in the form of organized terrorism like Al Qaeda, or it may be from individual terrorists who simply hate all Americans.

My hope and prayers are that our military will soon prevail in Iraq with minimal loss of additional lives for both our soldiers and the innocent people of Iraq. I also pray for the timely reconstruction of Iraq, establishment of a fair and just Iraqi government, and development of a healthy economy in that ravaged country. Then, the citizens of Iraq will have considerably better lives, and the risks of terrorism throughout the world will be reduced. Now, back to my initial question. Do you conclude that

I am unpatriotic and do not support our men and women in the military because I did not support President Bush and his decision to wage war against Iraq? Before you wrap yourself in the flag, put on your cloak of self-righteousness, and say yes, please answer this question. Did you support President Clinton and his administration, and if you did not, were you unpatriotic? Do not question my patriotism, and I will not question yours.

Let us look briefly at possible hypocrisy of the Bush administration and Republican Congress in the matter of support for our men and women in the military. At the start of the war in Iraq, the Republican House of Representatives passed a resolution declaring their support for our soldiers in Iraq. One would assume that support also applied to our many veterans, would you not agree? Within hours, however, the House passed a bill slashing veterans' benefits. We know veterans' benefits are not included in the defense budget, and they are not one of the entitlement programs, hence Congress has control of them. All that happened during the time Congress was crafting a huge tax cut bill to benefit primarily rich people and large corporations, and as they were also busy passing legislation allocating billions of dollars in funding for the war in Iraq. President Bush endorsed all of those actions. So, a Republican Congress and a Republican administration wrapped themselves in the flag, proclaimed support for our troops, and then slashed benefits for veterans and our wounded and maimed soldiers returning from Iraq. To me, that is hypocrisy in its worst form.

Throughout the Iraq conflict, the Bush administration has tried to control and manipulate news reports out of Iraq. Photographs of flag-draped coffins for soldiers returning from Iraq have been strictly forbidden. The Bush team does not want the American people to see the real cost of the war being waged in Iraq. Their motto is, "out of sight, out of mind," and it has worked for the most part. They also have strict rules about what journalists embedded with our military units can report about the war, and they try to suppress any news that is not favorable and not in agreement with the administration's claims about the progress of the war. The Bush team wants only positive news about Iraq to reach the American public, and they refuse to acknowledge that things are not going well there. President Bush ought to level with the American people. He should admit his mistakes about justification for invasion of Iraq, his lack of planning for the postwar reconstruction effort, his failure to plan for a committed and a very capable insurgency, his failure to grasp the magnitude and associated high costs of the war, and his lack of a viable exit strategy. American citizens are forgiving if they are told the truth. However, do not expect such an admission from an administration that refuses to acknowledge mistakes.

We constantly see President Bush and his inner circle posing at military installations with our troops and the flag as a backdrop. They keep telling us our soldiers support the war and want to finish the job in Iraq. They even pick out individual troops who express their support for the war and their desire to complete the mission. But, how do our soldiers in Iraq really feel about the war and the progress we are making there? Zogby International and LeMoyne College conducted the first poll of our men and women currently serving in Iraq, and the results of that poll were released at the end of February, 2006. The soldiers were asked several concise and straightforward questions, with no attempt by the pollsters to skew the results. They were asked,

"How long should U.S. troops stay in Iraq?" Seventy-two percent said they should be pulled out within a year, whereas only twenty-three percent stated they should stay as long as necessary. So, less than one-fourth of our troops in Iraq agree with President Bush's position. And, of those who wanted to pull out within a year, twenty-nine percent said we should pull out immediately.

The Bush team keeps telling us the insurgency in Iraq is driven by terrorists coming into Iraq from other countries. The implication is that the insurgency could be stopped if foreign fighters could be kept out. A majority of the soldiers polled, however, believe the insurgency consists primarily of Iraqi Sunnis. Only twenty-six percent of our troops believe the insurgency in Iraq would cease if the flow of terrorists into Iraq was stopped. Another key question to our soldiers in Iraq was what they thought it would take to control the insurgency. Two-thirds of them responded that we would have to double the number of American troops in Iraq. That essentially means the war in Iraq is not winnable, because the Bush administration is certainly not willing to double our troop strength there. Our soldiers in Iraq have spoken, so how will our president respond? Do not expect any change in tactics or rhetoric by the inept and stubborn Bush administration.

Just a few months subsequent to the start of the war, shortly after Baghdad was overrun by our military, and before Saddam Hussein was captured in his rathole, President Bush stood on the deck of the USS Abraham Lincoln aircraft carrier and declared, "Mission Accomplished." In that orchestrated appearance, in which he landed on the deck of an anchored aircraft carrier just a short distance from our shore, our triumphant president proclaimed that the Saddam Hussein regime had been toppled and implied that the conflict was essentially over. That highly publicized event was a stark reminder that President Bush and his inner circle did not grasp the gravity of the situation in Iraq. After almost three more years of fierce fighting, in excess of two thousand American soldiers killed, and more than 18,000 of our troops wounded, the Bush team still doesn't get it. They keep telling us everything is going well in Iraq according to plan. How much longer will a gullible American public tolerate such a whitewash job? Unfortunately, the President's faithful supporters are just as unwilling to admit that the Iraq war has been a fiasco from the start and that the Bush administration has botched the whole operation. They stubbornly go along with whatever their president tells them; he can speak no untruth. That is the penalty we pay for having such a bitterly divided country.

Six recently retired generals, at least three of which served in Iraq before their retirement, have criticized Secretary of Defense Donald Rumsfeld's conduct of the war in Iraq, and they have called for his resignation. The generals' basic complaint is that Secretary Rumsfeld and his aides ignored advice from his commanders and made military decisions that were unwise. Some of the generals say the invasion of Iraq was ill-advised, that it was peripheral to the war on terrorism. Others agree with the unilateral invasion of Iraq but question the way the war has been handled by Secretary Rumsfeld. Defenders of the Bush administration dismiss the generals' criticism, saying active commanders in Iraq have not spoken out against the conduct of the war. What they refuse to admit, however, is that active military officers must refrain from criticizing their civilian leaders, and if they do so, they put their careers at risk.

We hear about the number of American troops killed in Iraq, we see totals for those wounded, and we see television images of those soldiers who have been badly wounded and maimed in Iraq. We also hear daily accounts of how many Iraqi policemen and Iraqi soldiers have been killed and wounded, along with the number of Iraqi civilians killed and wounded. What we do not hear, though, is the total number of Iraqi casualties for the entire war, including those innocent civilians killed by American forces during the initial push into Iraq and those killed in insurgency operations during the last three years. That total number of Iraqi casualties must be staggering, most likely in the tens of thousands range if not higher. And, a majority of them were innocent civilians, caught in a war not of their choosing.

Our nation's conduct of the war in Iraq, and to some extent in Afghanistan, has tarnished our country's image around the globe. The entire world has observed newspaper photographs and television images of our troops abusing detainees at Abu Ghraib prison. We have held detainees for months, and even years, without charging them, and we have kept innocent Iraqis in detention camps and prisons for months or years. We hear reports of our government agencies sending prisoners on secret flights to other countries where torture is commonplace. That illegal detention and abuse of prisoners have been condoned and encouraged by the Bush administration. Those actions are not the manner of prisoner treatment that has earned the respect of other nations for America over the last one hundred years. Our country has always treated prisoners of war the way we would want our soldiers to be treated if they were captured. Our nation has always been perceived as just and humane in our treatment of prisoners of war. That has all changed, however, under the Bush administration. What right does America have now to demand that our troops be treated humanely if they fall into enemy hands? Where is the outrage that should be shown by our citizens over the abusive treatment of prisoners in Iraq and elsewhere? And, where are the objections of the holier-than-thou religious right over abuse and torture of detainees by our military and intelligence agencies? Perhaps we see a bit of hypocrisy in their inaction on the prisoner abuse issue.

We were told by the Bush administration that revenues from Iraqi oil exports would fund postwar reconstruction in Iraq. Protection of Iraqi oil facilities was one area of planning apparently accomplished prior to our invasion of Iraq. It was expected that Saddam Hussein would set fire to the Iraqi oil fields in much the same way he did to those in Kuwait during the Gulf War. That did not take place, however, in Iraq. Initial production of oil after the invasion was promising, but then the insurgency took over. Insurgents and terrorists have repeatedly attacked oil facilities in Iraq throughout the last three years. They have blown up pipelines, ambushed tanker trucks, and damaged oil wells and production facilities. Oil production in Iraq has not reached a level sufficient to meet the country's own needs; Iraq is importing oil for its own use. The oil revenues promised by the Bush team have not materialized, and America is paying the huge bill for the postwar reconstruction in Iraq.

The cost of postwar reconstruction in Iraq has been a lot higher than anticipated by the Bush administration. Reconstruction progress has been slowed dramatically by insurgent and terrorist attacks, and the cost of security for reconstruction projects has escalated. Many reconstruction projects have been plagued by shoddy workmanship and work that was never completed. Lucrative no-bid contracts to individuals and companies favored by the Bush administration have also driven the overall costs up. Lack of adequate inspections, or fraudulent sign-off of jobs not completed, have added to the cost woes of the reconstruction work in Iraq. A few important reconstruction projects have been completed, but there is much more to be done. The high level of ongoing insurgency and terrorist activity will surely result in even more reconstruction work as time goes by. The Bush administration has not provided a realistic estimate of the final reconstruction bill, but we can be sure it will be significantly higher than the total they have projected.

Fraud and corruption have been running rampant in Iraq, with inflated no-bid contracts being given to favored corporations and contractors. Price gouging, especially for gasoline imported from Kuwait, has been commonplace, and the military is billed for a lot of work never completed. For example, thousands of meals that were never delivered were included in invoices presented to our forces in Iraq. American and Iraqi businessmen have received lucrative contracts and very large sums of cash to fund various rebuilding projects. In addition, military personnel have had control of vast amounts of cash to pay for reconstruction work. There is minimal oversight for a large number of these projects, and tens of millions of dollars are unaccounted for. Stacks of $100 bills are routinely kept in unlocked desks and cabinets, with ready access to many individuals. It is thus no surprise much of that "loose money" has been spent for personal items such as expensive cars, fine jewelry, airplanes, computer equipment, expensive weaponry, and even real estate. A few individuals have been charged with fraud and corruption, and others are under investigation. We are probably looking at the tip of the iceberg, and there are most likely a multitude of guilty individuals and businesses that will never be charged.

Extreme partisanship and bitter division existed in America before the Bush administration initiated the Iraq war, but that polarization of our country has increased substantially as a result of the three-year conflict in Iraq. Many of our citizens who were opposed to the unilateral invasion of Iraq are agonizing over what we should do now. They believe our nation has an obligation to clean up the mess in Iraq before we leave. Their attitude is, "We broke it, so we should fix it," and rightfully so. It would also be detrimental to the security and interests of our country if we left Iraq in the state of chaos it is in now. That is why it is so important for the Bush administration to develop a viable exit strategy for Iraq. Both the American people and the Iraqi people deserve to know what we plan to accomplish in Iraq and how we are going to do it. But, do not expect anything meaningful and realistic from such an incompetent administration.

I realize many of the readers of this book disagree with my assessment of the conflict in Iraq. I am sure a lot of you consider President Bush (and by extension, his inner circle of advisors) to be an honest, ethical, credible, and competent leader. For those loyal supporters of our president, I have a few probing and challenging questions. Did you believe President Bush when he told us Iraq possessed weapons of mass destruction? We all know that statement has been proven false. And, did you believe him when he stated prior to invading Iraq that close ties existed between Saddam Hussein and Al Qaeda terrorists, that Iraq had a part in the 9/11 terrorists attack on America? That claim has also been proven incorrect. Did you believe our president when he told us the war in Iraq would last no longer than two years maximum? The conflict has been going on over three years, with no end on the horizon. Further, did you believe him when he insisted the war in Iraq would cost about $60 billion? The direct cost of the war is approaching $400 billion and still rising. Did you believe President Bush when he stood on the deck of the USS Abraham Lincoln in May, 2003, and proclaimed, "Mission Accomplished," implying that the war with Iraq was essentially finished? Our war with Iraq is still going strong over three years later. Did you believe him in 2005 when he said the insurgency was on its last legs? The insurgency is alive and well in 2006 and still growing. Did you believe President Bush when he told us in 2000 that he was a uniter rather than a divider? America is more bitterly divided now than it has been since the Civil War almost 150 years ago. I do not know about you, but I believe in the old adage, "Experience is the best teacher." Experience tells me President Bush is not credible and certainly is not a competent leader.

If everyone would look honestly at what has transpired the last three years in this country with regard to Iraq, examine the validity of their own beliefs about Iraq, resolve to be more respectful of the views of others, and be willing to compromise on some of the issues that divide our nation, I believe some of the polarization and bitterness could be eliminated in this country.

CHAPTER 5

The Homeland Security Farce

—∽∼∽—

The surprise September 11, 2001, terrorist attack on our country prompted many politicians to demand that a single government agency be established to protect our nation from another attack. The initial push for such a central agency was primarily by Democrats, with the Bush administration and most Republicans being opposed. As public pressure mounted, however, the Bush administration and Republican Congress acquiesced and initiated their own plan for a unified homeland security agency that would report directly to the president. That central agency would be responsible for prevention of, preparation for, and response to national emergencies and disasters. The driving force in establishing the Department of Homeland Security was prevention of another terrorist attack similar to that of 9/11, but the department would also be responsible for responding to natural disasters such as floods, hurricanes, and earthquakes.

The concept of one central federal agency being responsible for the security of our country is sound. That should eliminate competition between various federal agencies with regard to responsibilities and funding. Communication and coordination between the individual agencies should also be improved if all agencies are controlled by one official. A significant amount of the bureaucratic red tape should certainly be eliminated with one central agency in charge, and response times for emergencies ought to be much shorter. Planning for, and prevention of, disasters such as floods and hurricanes should be enhanced because all responsible federal identities would be working together under one leader. The overall operational cost of one all-encompassing security agency ought to be less than the combined costs of several separate agencies responsible for specific areas of national security. Redundant administrative functions and duplicate operations could be eliminated. Having all national security functions reporting to the president would enable him to cut through red tape in the case of a dire national emergency.

The Bush administration and Republican-controlled Congress did establish the Department of Homeland Security (DHS), under a homeland security czar reporting directly to the president. Although conceptually sound, combining all national security functions under one roof did create a few severe practical problems. The DHS is huge and unwieldy, and effective implementation of such a large organization does require a very long time period, measured in years. Coordination of all federal security functions with state and local agencies proved to be a tremendous task as well, one which requires a long time period to accomplish. Then, there is the problem of allocating resources and funding to various areas of homeland security. Sufficient resources must be in place for prevention of terrorist attacks, but adequate resources must also be provided for responses to potential and actual natural disasters. In their rush to prevent another terrorist attack on our country, the Bush administration short-changed those agencies responsible for responding to natural disasters, especially the Federal Emergency Management Agency (FEMA).

A fundamental but wrong political decision by the Bush administration amplified all the other problems. Rather than select individuals with emergency management experience or those with extensive experience in intelligence work for key slots in the new Department of Homeland Security, the Bush team made what are essentially political appointments. Individuals were nominated for important positions within the DHS because of their financial and political support of the president and because of their ideologies that were in agreement with those of the Bush team. A prime example of such a person being selected for a key position although he had virtually no related experience is Michael Brown, director of FEMA. Mr. Brown had no emergency management experience, yet he was given the job to head up FEMA. Filling important government positions on the basis of cronyism or political rewards is bad policy, but that is the mode of operation in the Bush administration.

Many experts within the emergency management community believe FEMA should not have been included in the Department of Homeland Security. Manpower and funding were stripped from FEMA and given to those agencies more concerned with terrorist attacks on America and its overseas interests. Terrorism had the undivided attention of the Bush administration, so they turned a deaf ear to any requests or warnings having to do with natural disasters. Instead, all available manpower, money, and expertise were devoted to combating terrorism. FEMA was thus left with limited capability to identify potential disasters, prepare for them, and respond to major events. States and cities were thus left with the responsibility to prepare for natural disasters such as hurricanes and floods and to respond to them. Obviously, states and cities do not have the necessary resources to handle events of major proportion, such as that of Hurricane Katrina that battered New Orleans and the Gulf Coast in 2005.

Hurricane Katrina was a monster storm that caused catastrophic flooding in the city of New Orleans and extensive damage all along the Louisiana and Mississippi Gulf Coast. That storm occurred four years after the 9/11 terrorist attack, so our nation should have been prepared for such an emergency. There was really no way to prevent a lot of the havoc wrought by Katrina on the Gulf Coast, but our government's response to it should have been much quicker and with greater resources. A lot of finger-pointing has taken place between city, state, and federal officials regarding who was to blame and who should have done what, therefore it is quite difficult to determine who dropped the ball.

Four days after Hurricane Katrina struck New Orleans and the levees failed, President Bush declared, "I don't think anybody anticipated the breach of the levees." Was the President truthful in his explanation of the reason for the slow response by the federal government to the huge storm? A video surfaced some six months after Katrina that clearly proved President Bush was not honest with the American people and the survivors in New Orleans. A video conference was held the day before the storm pushed ashore, between FEMA chief Michael Brown, the Secretary of the Department of Homeland Security, Michael Chernoff, and the White House. President Bush was plainly informed by Michael Brown and others that a giant storm was bearing down on New Orleans, that the city levees could fail, that if they did fail the city would suffer catastrophic flooding, and that adequate preparation had not been made for such an event. The aftermath of Hurricane Katrina is only one of numerous occasions wherein President Bush has been untruthful with our country and refused to accept any blame for his mismanagement and bad decisions. The president's loyal supporters steadfastly maintain he is honest and truthful with the American people. What will it take to open their eyes?

One thing is perfectly clear, though. Everyone had ample warning that a potentially catastrophic storm was bearing down on New Orleans and the Gulf Coast. Perhaps the city of New Orleans should have taken earlier and stronger action to evacuate the city, but we do not know how many people would have refused to leave their homes. Also, the states of Louisiana and Mississippi probably could have brought in additional resources to prepare for the aftermath of the powerful hurricane. But, state resources for a catastrophe of that magnitude are woefully inadequate, especially with so many of our National Guard troops and equipment deployed to Iraq. The only agency with sufficient manpower, equipment, and money to respond to a disaster of such magnitude is the federal government, but FEMA was notably absent before Katrina hit the Gulf Coast and for several days afterward. Why was that?

A special committee in the House of Representatives investigated the mishandling of the response to Hurricane Katrina. That special committee consisted of eleven Republicans, so their report was not partisan bashing by Democrats. The report was in all likelihood easier on the Bush administration than it could have been, because it was Republicans attacking Republicans, and that is something we seldom see. Among those questioned by the special committee was Michael Brown, former head of FEMA, who was removed from that position because of the poor response by FEMA in the aftermath of Hurricane Katrina. A concurrent White House report on the government's response to the devastation caused by Katrina came to similar conclusions. However, the White House report was not as critical of individuals at the management level of the Department of Homeland Security and FEMA.

The report from the special House committee did not place the blame for the government's miserable performance in responding to the Hurricane Katrina disaster on any particular individual, but the implications are clear: (1) The magnitude of Hurricane Katrina and its general path were known several days before it slammed ashore just East of New Orleans; (2) Catastrophic failure of the New Orleans levees in the event of such a strong storm had been predicted for years; (3) The potential magnitude of destruction along the Gulf Coast in the event of a major hurricane like Katrina was well known; (4) The White House, and President Bush personally, was informed of the collapse of the New Orleans levees a few hours after the storm hit the city; (5) Extreme flooding in the event the levee system failed had been predicted for many years; (6) FEMA had made virtually no preparation to deal with flooding and wind damage along the Gulf Coast; (7) The magnitude of the devastation caused by Hurricane Katrina overwhelmed state and local emergency service agencies; (8) The federal government, including the Bush administration, did not grasp the magnitude of the problems caused by the monster storm; (9) The required initiative and leadership within the federal government were not provided before the hurricane struck the Gulf Coast or in its aftermath; (10) President Bush was ultimately responsible for providing that initiative and leadership, and he failed to do so; (11) Any meaningful response to Hurricane Katrina by the federal government did not come until several days after the storm came ashore; and (12) The federal government's miserable response to the hurricane was inexcusable.

The aftermath of Hurricane Katrina brought to light a critical problem in America, that of millions of our citizens living in abject poverty. A majority of those people stranded in flooded sections of New Orleans were not able to flee the city if they had wanted to. Most of them did not own cars, they possessed no money to pay for transportation out of the city or for lodging elsewhere, and many residents were unable to walk a great distance. We can easily blame them for not leaving their homes when evacuation of the city was ordered, but they did not have the ability to do so. FEMA should have provided transportation so those impoverished residents could leave, and arrangements should have been made to provide them with lodging until the storm had passed. Those people stranded in New Orleans had no food, no water, no lodging, no bathroom facilities, no security, and no health care for days, so it is not surprising they became unruly and turned to looting. What would you have done if your family was stranded under such terrible conditions? Would you not have broken into a store or business to find provisions for your hungry and thirsty children? Our nation did show compassion on Hurricane Katrina evacuees by providing them with lodging, clothing, food, and other necessary provisions in the aftermath of that huge storm. But, what are we doing to help people in similar impoverished neighborhoods throughout America? You would like to think our country is reaching out to help them escape from such a terrible environment. Instead, the Bush administration and Republican Congress have slashed spending for social programs designed to help such poor people, and at the same time have given huge tax cuts and subsidies to our richest citizens and large corporations.

The absence of a timely response to Hurricane Katrina by our federal government is a clear indication that our country is not prepared to deal with a catastrophic terrorist attack. Our Department of Homeland Security was unprepared for a well defined disaster at a known location, with several days advance notice, so how can we say we are prepared for an unexpected attack at an undisclosed location with no advance notice? All the Bush administration's rhetoric about being prepared for another terrorist attack is meaningless. Our nation

has spent billions of dollars creating a homeland security bureaucracy that is woefully inadequate. Perhaps
a fresh start with new experienced leadership, clear
objectives, elimination of politics in the program, and
oversight by a truly bipartisan and knowledgeable
congressional committee would yield a Department of
Homeland Security capable of protecting our country. I
cannot visualize that happening, though, with the inept
Bush administration in command.

Protecting our country against terrorism is a tall
order, considering the minimal control we have of our
borders and the ease with which people can travel into
and out of our nation. Also, our lifestyle is not condu-
cive to effective protection against terrorism. Capable
terrorists would have no significant problems in
bringing all types of weapons and bomb making material into our country, and they would have ready access
to oil refineries, transportation centers, water and food
supplies, financial centers, and other locations where
multitudes of people congregate. The Department of
Homeland Security has spent billions of dollars to make
our commercial airports "secure," but only a small
percentage of imported containers at our seaports are

inspected. Our border control agencies are unable to effectively control the flow of illegal aliens, narcotics, and weapons into our country. Measures could be taken to make our borders more secure, and better surveillance could be implemented at critical locations around our nation, but the costs would be prohibitive and the overall effectiveness would be questionable.

The most effective way to reduce terrorism, I believe, is to address its source and at the same time develop a more effective intelligence network. It is imperative that our nation work with other countries, including Muslim countries, to identify measures that could be taken to reduce hatred of America by Islam extremists. Invading an Arab country is certainly not the best way to go; our unilateral invasion of Iraq has proven that point. We cannot deal effectively with Islam extremists until our state department understands the Islam religion and the Muslim culture, a knowledge severely lacking in the Bush administration. I certainly do not know all that is going on in our intelligence community to combat terrorism, but it appears to me the one important ingredient missing is infiltration of terrorist networks by our agents. That is the only way, I believe, to find out their specific plans and then stop would-be terrorists before they reach our soil.

Effective preparation for, and timely response to, natural disasters or terrorist attacks require close coordination between the Department of Homeland Security and state and local agencies. The cost of not having that close coordination was clearly demonstrated in the aftermath of Hurricane Katrina. Simply passing unfunded mandates and policies down to the states and raising the level of terrorist alerts are not sufficient. The federal government must fund initiatives aimed at reducing terrorism and improving our response to potential attacks. And, raising the terrorist alert level must be in response to a real threat, not just an action to accomplish a political goal. We all remember the frequent terrorist alerts in 2004, which coincided with our last presidential campaign. President Bush's political advisors realized his reelection hinged on keeping the terrorism issue front and center until after the election. Hence, we saw increased alerts before the election and relatively few afterward. Using our nation's security as a political tool in such a manner is reprehensible, but it worked; President Bush was reelected by a slim margin.

Rather than fund all homeland security mandates passed down to the states and cities, our Republican Congress has used a large part of the homeland security budget to reward representatives and senators who support the Republican Party's positions on key issues. Districts with Congressmen and Congresswomen who support the Republican leadership and the Bush administration are more likely to receive funding for homeland security initiatives, although many of those districts do not encompass a valid security threat. Much of the money is spent on projects not related to homeland security. That is what we call earmarks, or pork-barrel funding. Once again, the Republican Party is playing politics with our nation's security.

Wherever you find federal money, you will also find fraud and corruption in the Bush administration. The Department of Homeland Security is no different. Contracts are directed to those corporations and businesses favored by the Republican Party and the Bush administration, which translates into those who support them financially. Minimal oversight by either Congress or the department leads to price gouging and work not completed. The aftermath of Hurricane Katrina was a prime example of fraud and corruption in the Department of Homeland Security. Lucrative no-bid contracts were awarded to favored contractors, price gouging was commonplace, there was minimal oversight for most projects, and much of the money went to undeserving recipients.

I believe two significant changes are needed in the Department of Homeland Security. The first is to separate FEMA from the department, including separate funding for FEMA and staffing it with key people possessing extensive experience in emergency management. Preparation for, and response to, natural disasters are appreciably different from that of combating terrorism, so those two tasks should be separated. Keep in mind, though, that close coordination and cooperation between FEMA and the Department of Homeland Security is a necessity. And, there will be some degree of overlap in the work they do.

The second change is more drastic because of the political climate in America. The Department of Homeland Security and FEMA must be truly bipartisan. That means key positions should be filled with equal numbers of Republicans and Democrats, and all nominees to those key positions should be selected and approved by a bipartisan congressional committee, with White House input. Such a process would tend to eliminate the current politicizing of the Department of Homeland Security by the Bush administration. In addition, a bipartisan oversight committee (which could be the same committee) having equal numbers of Republicans and Democrats must have authority to ensure efficient and timely performance of homeland security and FEMA operations. That oversight committee should have the responsibility to ascertain that adequate planning and preparation for emergencies are in place, and that communication, cooperation, and coordination are maintained between FEMA and the Department of Homeland Security. The congressional oversight committee should also take whatever steps necessary to root out fraud and corruption. In my opinion, the Bush administration's mismanagement of homeland security has made such a drastic change necessary.

One would think homeland security is a bipartisan concern, an issue that would not lead to bitter division in our country. That is not the case for the Department of Homeland Security, however, because it has been politicized from its inception by the Bush administration. The Bush team has tried to cast the invasion of Iraq as an integral part of the larger war against terrorism, but that is an invalid claim. The Republican Party and our president, with the support of the religious right, have combined the war against terrorism, the conflict with Iraq, and homeland security together in a common package. And, they accuse anyone opposed to any part of that package of being unpatriotic. Such a judgmental attitude toward any person who opposed the unilateral invasion of Iraq has caused an increase in polarization and division in our nation.

CHAPTER 6

Big Money is in Control

—m—

The Republican Party has always exhibited favoritism toward big business and wealthy individuals, at the expense of the working class and poor people. That trend has steadily increased over the last twenty or so years, with our nation's wealth being transferred from the lower and middle classes of our society to large corporations and the wealthiest twenty percent of our population. That process was slowed to some extent during the eight-year Clinton administration, but it has rapidly accelerated under President Bush and a Republican Congress. Their spending decisions, tax policies, environmental policies, trade decisions, ethics rules, and other regulations and enforcement guidelines always benefit rich people and large corporations, to the detriment of everyone else.

If policies of the Republican Party favor only the wealthiest twenty percent of our population, how have the Republicans gained firm control of both the Executive Branch and the Legislative Branch of our government? Why has our country elected a Republican president and a Republican Congress in both 2000 and 2004? That is a very good question, one that does not have a simple and straightforward answer. Let us first remember, though, that only slightly greater than fifty percent of all eligible citizens vote in our nation, whereas almost all wealthy Americans vote, and they vote overwhelmingly Republican. That means less than fifty percent of the lower-income and middle-income eligible voters actually vote, so the Republican Party wins elections if they garner more than forty percent of the lower-class and middle-class votes. The Republican Party has been able to do that, beginning with the 2000 presidential election, but their winning margins have been extremely narrow.

How has the Republican Party been able to capture such a large share of votes from our middle class and lower class if their agenda is so heavily tilted toward the wealthy and big business? Their success can be attributed, I believe, to four major factors. First and foremost is the sizable money advantage enjoyed by the Republican Party. Wealthy individuals and large corporations contribute heavily to Republican candidates at all levels of our political system, whereas a majority of the supporters of the Democratic Party are not able to contribute as heavily. It is obvious that wealthy people and big businesses prefer to keep Republicans in power so they can continue to enjoy a political system tilted in their favor. That money advantage translates into more television, radio, newspaper, and direct mail political ads for Republican candidates, as well as greater numbers of paid campaign workers, telephone banks, and computer networks.

A second major factor is the overwhelming support of the Republican Party by the religious right. The religious right consists for the most part of highly motivated and committed citizens who have very strong beliefs about religious and moral issues such as abortion, homosexuality, prayer in public schools, euthanasia, and gay marriage. They support candidates who agree with them on those hot-button issues, and they virtually ignore other important social, fiscal, and environmental issues. The religious right is comprised of outspoken activists, committed workers, and consistent voters, so they are an important part of the Republican Party. As discussed earlier, conservative Republicans have embraced the religious right, or social conservatives, incorporating their religious and moral views into the Republican Party agenda. By pandering to the religious right, the Republican Party has gained a sizable and reliable voting block, even though the Party's fiscal policies and tax policies are actually detrimental to most of the individuals that make up the religious right. That is of little concern to social conservatives, however, because they vote on the basis of those hot-button issues such as abortion and gay marriage. The Republican Party also embraces other special interest groups who have very narrow agendas. One such group is the National Rifle Association (NRA) which is made up of gun enthusiasts. NRA members, as well as many nonmembers who are sympathetic to their cause, are gun owners who strongly oppose any form of gun control, and they are quite often one-issue voters who support or oppose a candidate on the basis of his or her view on gun control.

Therefore, gun enthusiasts vote for Republican candidates by a large margin.

The third major factor stems from selfishness and greed that permeate our society today. The Republican Party is responsible to a large extent for that greed, and it has certainly learned how to capitalize on it. Wealthy individuals and large corporations enthusiastically support tax policies and fiscal policies that favor them, so a large majority of our wealthier citizens support Republican candidates. The Republican Party gains support of middle-income and lower-income voters by holding out a carrot; they offer one-time tax rebates to all taxpayers, and they claim their tax cuts "put money back into the pockets of everyone who pays taxes." What they do not tell us is that a vast majority of the overall tax cuts and tax subsidies go to the richest ten percent of our population, and that those tax cuts lead to huge budget deficits. The Republicans know many people will choose nominal tax cuts and tax rebates for themselves, even though the overall tax structure is detrimental to our country. Personal greed triumphs over reason.

Huge budget deficits caused by tax cuts and tax subsidies for the wealthy are not new for the Republican

Party. Similar tax cuts for the wealthy under President Ronald Reagan resulted in very large budget deficits. The Reagan tax policy was called supply side economics by Republicans, but it was referred to as "voodoo economics" by the first President Bush, and his name for it seems more appropriate. Nonetheless, voters in this country are gullible enough, and greedy enough, to buy into such unrealistic tax policies. President Bush's economic policy is a rerun of the voodoo economics referred to by his father, but he is getting away with it. Selfish and greedy voters condone and support unfair tax cuts and tax subsidies, and they have no qualms about passing mountainous debt down to their children and grandchildren. Once again, greed and selfishness win out over austerity and common sense.

The fourth major factor contributing to the Republican Party's success in winning elections is their unequaled expertise in the use of negative politics. Negative campaigning, or mud slinging, has always been a part of our political system, but Republicans have refined the art of negative campaigning. Their willingness to demonize opposition candidates has no boundary. Huge Republican campaign war chests and wealthy supporters willing to fund expensive negative ads enable the Republican Party to launch large campaigns to discredit Democratic candidates. Such campaign ads are filled with innuendos, misrepresentations, and outright lies, but they work. Republican candidates are elected. The Republican Party and their financial supporters have accused decorated, wounded, and maimed war veterans of being fakes and cowards. Such use of negative politics is disgraceful, but it is the norm for the Republican Party.

A good measure of the greed and corruption prevalent in our society is the large number of corporate scandals we have witnessed in the last few years. All of us have heard about the failures of giant corporations like Enron and World Com, but many other large and small corporations have similar problems. Greedy corporate managers collect huge salaries and bonuses for themselves, they misrepresent corporate profits to keep their stock prices inflated, and they give generously to politicians to gain favor in passage of bills that benefit their companies. Then, when one of these corporations goes under, their employees, retirees, investors, and stockholders are left holding the bag. Tens of thousands of employees and retirees with Enron and World Com lost their life savings when those two corporations failed. A large number of those corporate scandals are playing out in our judicial system at the present time. A number of financial and accounting institutions have agreed to large fines and settlements for their parts in "cooking the books," quite a few corporate officers have pleaded guilty for their contributions to the scandals, others have been convicted and are serving prison time, and still others are either awaiting trials or going through trials. Meanwhile, their investors, employees, retirees, and stockholders are waiting for their meager share of whatever corporate assets are left.

A number of high-level executives responsible for those large corporate scandals were key financial supporters and good pals of the Bush administration. For example, it is widely believed Enron executives worked with Vice President Dick Cheney in crafting his energy bill, but Mr. Cheney has refused to reveal the names of energy industry representatives who participated in that effort. It doesn't require a rocket scientist to figure out who the energy bill would benefit most if it indeed was written by executives in the energy industry. That seems to be the standard operating procedure, however, for the Bush administration; those industries most affected by legislation are permitted to influence, or even write, the laws. Another example of such skulduggery is the Medicare Prescription Drug bill passed by Congress in 2005. Lobbyists and representatives for pharmaceutical and insurance companies were heavily involved in crafting that bill and getting it passed by Congress. The end result was a Medicare Prescription Drug Program that provides minimal benefits for our senior citizens, but one that dishes out billions of dollars in subsidies to the pharmaceutical and insurance industries. Money does indeed buy influence in the Republican Congress and Bush administration.

Money was not such a major concern for political campaigns in years past, especially before the advent of television as a major source of news. Name identification, party affiliation, and party platform were primary factors for voters, and most voters consistently supported candidates from either the Republican or the Democratic Parties. People relied heavily on radio networks for news and for information about the candidates, and personal appearances by the candidates were the most effective means of reaching voters. Television changed all of that, however, and political action committees (PACs) burst into the political scene. Large amounts of money were required for political television ads, and PACs became the primary source for that money. Fund raising thus became the greatest concern for anyone running for public office, and effective statewide and national campaigns now require astronomical sums of money. The PACs that contribute big bucks to get candidates elected want something in return for their support, and politicians know they must give those big contributors what they want if they are to be reelected. Politicians are therefore bought by large contributors; big money is in control.

A majority of the money contributed in earlier political campaigns was given directly to the candidates, and they controlled the way the money was spent and the contents of the political ads it bought. That kind of direct contribution was referred to as hard money; it was given to the candidates, and it was controlled by their campaigns. Strict rules have been established to govern the amount of money that can be given directly to the candidates by an individual or a PAC, so a different method of contributing to campaigns was sought by politicians. Soft money thus entered the political arena. That is money spent by an individual or an organization to support a candidate or a political Party, but spending of that money cannot be coordinated in any way with the candidate and his or her campaign. The allowable amount of soft money is essentially unlimited, so the overall level of spending in political campaigns has increased substantially in the last few years because of that soft money.

Money draws a crowd in politics, so the role of lobbyists became a major factor as special-interest groups attempted to influence our elected officials. Corporations, industries, organizations, and other special-interest groups have always hired people to represent them in Washington and the state capitals. The primary function of these representatives, or lobbyists, is to get the ear of Congressmen and Congresswomen in Washington, administration officials, or members of our state legislatures and convince them to pass laws and regulations that benefit their clients. Intense pressure is applied on members of Congress to accumulate larger and larger sums of money to ensure reelection, so our

Congressmen and Congresswomen have become more susceptible to being bought off by lobbyists. That is, they will write legislation to benefit their largest campaign contributors, even to the point of allowing lobbyists to participate in the writing of the laws and regulations. A prime example of such unethical practice is the Medicare Prescription Drug Program that was written by Congress, with the help of representatives from pharmaceutical and insurance companies, and then railroaded through Congress in 2005. Another example is the administration energy bill crafted by Vice President Cheney, together with help of representatives from the energy industry. Our Republican-controlled Congress and the Bush administration always seem to cave in to well-heeled special-interest groups, to the detriment of the middle class, our poorer citizens, and senior adults.

Lobbyists and special-interest groups have developed and refined another unethical, and oftentimes illegal, means of gaining favor with politicians. They capitalize on the culture of greed and corruption inherent in Congress and our state governments by providing expense-paid trips and "working vacations" for our elected officials, their staffs, and their families.

Lobbyists put out significant sums of money to pay for outings to lavish hotels in Europe, golfing in prestigious clubs in Scotland, weekend hideaways in the Bahamas, tickets to major sporting events, dining in elite restaurants, and other such extravagant activities where politicians supposedly conduct "our business." Many of our politicians no longer represent their constituencies or consider what is best for our country. Instead, they do what is demanded of them by the special-interest groups and lobbyists who contribute big bucks to their campaign funds. Big money controls our national and state governments.

Both the Democratic Party and the Republican Party have been corrupted by the stream of big money flowing from lobbyists and special-interest groups, but it has been much more evident in the Republican Party. That is primarily because Republicans consistently favor wealthy people and large corporations, and that is where the big bucks are found. The Republican Party has always enjoyed an inherent advantage in campaign funding, but with control of the White House and both houses of Congress by Republicans, the Bush administration and Congress have tried to extend that advantage and make it permanent. Their basic goal is to render the Democratic Party powerless and thus transform our country into a one-party system of government with the Republican Party in control. That translates into a virtual dictatorship rather than a democracy, but a large number of our citizens are buying into it.

K Street in Washington is the address of many of the most powerful lobbyists in that city, and the number of registered lobbyists in our nation's capital has doubled in the first five years of the Bush administration. Lobbyists currently number about 35,000 in Washington. What is essentially a revolving door exists between our nation's capital and K Street, with retiring lawmakers moving into much more lucrative positions in lobbying firms. Former Congressmen-turned-lobbyists have a thorough understanding of the legislative process and unique access to their former colleagues. Former Congressmen and Congresswomen are allowed on the Senate and House floors during debate on bills, so they can talk with Representatives and Senators during that debate. They also have access to places frequented by lawmakers, such as gyms. Former Congressmen and Congresswomen therefore have an edge over other lobbyists.

Congressional Republicans, led by former House majority leader Tom DeLay, established what is referred to as the K Street Project. That was an attempt by Congressional Republicans to firm up their control of lobbyists. Their goal is to have only lobbyists with Republican views, which essentially means having only Republicans as lobbyists. To accomplish that feat, Republicans use intimidation and coercion to force lobbying firms to hire only Republicans. They deny access to Congressional Republicans by lobbying firms who do not go along with their directive. Under such an arrangement, Democratic incumbents have minimal access to the huge amounts of money controlled by the lobbyists, and Republican control of Congress can be perpetuated. These kinds of actions by the Republican Congress raise ethical and legal questions, and several investigations are currently underway. One Republican House member, Randy Cunningham, has pleaded guilty for accepting bribes and has been sentenced to prison. Tom DeLay was forced to relinquish his position as House majority leader after being indicted, he has announced his retirement from Congress, and he is now awaiting trial in Texas.

The best known lobbyist, and apparently the most powerful, is Jack Abramoff. He headed up a very large and effective lobbying network that ignored lobbyists' restrictions. One of Abramoff's close associates was Tom DeLay, and Abramoff claimed numerous Republican leaders as his friends, including President Bush. The extent of his lobbying operations is being investigated, but Abramoff and one of his lobbying partners, Michael Scanlon, have pleaded guilty to bribery and corruption charges and are cooperating with the ongoing investigation. Scanlon was also a former top aide to House Majority Leader Tom DeLay. It will be interesting to see how all these bribery and corruption investigations play out, but I am sure several incumbent Congressmen and Congresswomen are quite concerned, especially House Republicans.

The corruptive influence of big money is evident in the Republican legislative agenda. Tax cuts and subsidies pushed by the Bush administration and passed by the Republican Congress benefit wealthy people and large corporations. Those huge tax breaks for the wealthy account for a major portion of the record deficits run up by the Bush administration. The Republican legislative agenda is payback to the well-heeled special-interest groups who support them and come through with obscene campaign contributions. I am confident pharmaceutical companies and insurance companies are well pleased with the Medicare Prescription Drug Program which was developed for their benefit. That Medicare drug program is pure and simple payback to the insurance and pharmaceutical industries for their generous financial support of Republican candidates and causes.

Large corporations are equally pleased with the so-called tort reform and bankruptcy bills passed by the Republican Congress. The stated purposes of those bills were to reduce frivolous lawsuits and eliminate abuse of bankruptcy laws, but that was just a smokescreen to hide their real intentions. The tort reform legislation severely limits people's ability to sue corporations that have done them wrong, especially making it more difficult to win class-action lawsuits against companies. Think of the money corporations can save just on asbestos claims. The tort reform bill is not aimed, as claimed by Republicans, at overzealous lawyers who file frivolous lawsuits. It is aimed instead at attorneys who represent poorer plaintiffs, and it benefits corporate attorneys and their companies. The bankruptcy bill makes it much more difficult to file Chapter 7 bankruptcy, wherein individuals and businesses are allowed to write off their debts and start over. Instead, consumers are forced to pay off credit card loans at obscene interest rates and with large penalties, and in no way does the bill limit credit card companies' sleazy practice of soliciting clients and handing out credit cards indiscriminately with onerous interest rates. The credit card industry has been seeking limits on bankruptcy protection for a long time. Again, these unfair laws are payback to large corporations for their financial support of the Republican Party and its candidates.

In the rush to pass laws and regulations to benefit their wealthy constituents, the Bush administration and Republican Congress have virtually ignored potential harm to the environment. They refuse to acknowledge any man-caused global warming, and they manipulate, misrepresent, and even manufacture scientific data and reports to support their positions regarding the environment. Laws and regulations have been relaxed or rescinded to benefit oil companies, timber companies, mining companies, petrochemical companies, land developers, and other special-interest groups. As a result, the air we breathe is polluted, the water we drink is contaminated, our land is poisoned, the safety of our wildlife is at risk, and our pristine parks and land are altered. Needless to say, those polluting industries contribute heavily to Republican campaigns and causes.

Government oversight and control of industries affecting the environment are becoming less and less stringent under the Bush administration. Many of the environmental laws and regulations have been eliminated or relaxed, and funding for those agencies responsible for oversight has been cut back. The Bush administration has appointed people from various industries to head up government agencies responsible for controlling those same industries, so little effort is expended to eliminate unethical or illegal practices. Damage to the environment is thus not a major concern to the polluting industries. A byproduct of such lax control of industry is the sacrifice of employee safety. Numerous rules and regulations address employee safety, and when those guidelines are relaxed or not enforced, employees are at risk. Companies are routinely cited for not meeting employee safety requirements, but they are hardly ever penalized, so they seldom change their operating practices. We have been made acutely aware of that problem by recent coal mining accidents wherein several miners lost their lives. And, the companies involved had been cited repeatedly for safety violations, but they had done virtually nothing to eliminate the problems. Emphasis continues to be on bottom line profits rather than on employee safety.

The corrupting influence of big money in American politics has contributed to the extreme partisanship in our country. It is most obvious in Congress and in political campaigns, but the division stemming from greed and corruption in Washington has filtered down to every level of our society. The only way to reduce that polarization in America is to limit the amount of money that can be poured into political campaigns. But, do not hold your breath until our politicians develop the will and courage to take on that task.

CHAPTER 7

Executive Branch Power Grab

—∭—

A key to the success of our democracy has been the delicate balance of power between the Executive Branch, Legislative Branch, and Judicial Branch of our government. Our founding fathers recognized that without a balance of power a dictatorship could evolve, so they incorporated checks and balances into our Constitution and Bill of Rights. Our nation has always had some degree of tug-of-war between the Executive Branch and the Legislative Branch of our government, but the Judicial Branch has served as a moderating influence. Our Constitution identifies Congress as the limiter of presidential power, but Congress has not always assumed that authority, especially during those times when one political party had control of both Congress and the presidency.

A number of our past presidents have endeavored to assume greater power than that granted them by Congress and our Constitution; they have consistently strived to raise the bar on presidential powers. Attempts by presidents to usurp authority seem to be more prevalent during times of war or after other kinds of national emergencies, and a presidential power grab is driven quite often by an ideology or a partisan political agenda. The ready availability and strong influence of big money in politics have changed the dynamics of our democratic form of government. Our president now has the capability of using his bully pulpit, together with huge sums of special-interest money, to communicate a biased message to the people, to discredit his critics, to silence opposition in his own political party, and to intimidate Congress into turning a blind eye to his abuse of presidential power. Party allegiance also precludes most members of Congress from standing up to the president if he is one of their own. Party loyalty has precedence over what may be best for our country.

The Bush administration has taken abuse of presidential power to a new level. It is a presidency driven by ideology, rooted in religious and political fundamentalism, supported by vast amounts of special-interest money, biased toward wealthy people and big business, void of concern and compassion for the downtrodden, and rife with corruption and incompetence. The Bush team's essential goal is to solidify and perpetuate Republican control of our nation by minimizing the Democratic Party's clout in Congress, eliminating funding options for Democratic political campaigns, making it more difficult for Democratic-leaning people groups to vote, using state redistricting as a political tool to ensure reelection of Republican incumbents to Congress and the state legislatures, reducing Democratic Congressmen's access to lobbyists and their big bucks, giving huge tax cuts and tax subsidies to wealthy people and large corporations, and stacking the Supreme Court and other federal courts with judges sympathetic to Republican causes. The Republican Congress and the Bush administration are willing to use any means necessary, legal or not, to maintain control of our country. The large number of convictions, indictments, and ongoing criminal investigations of prominent Republican politicians and lobbyists paint a portrait of greed and corruption within the Bush administration and Republican Congress.

Prior to the 9/11 terrorist attacks on our country, the Bush administration was struggling. Their domestic agenda was unpopular, the economy was on life support, and President Bush's approval rating was dismal. Then, the American people rallied around President Bush as he led our country into a justified war against Al Qaeda and the Taliban regime in Afghanistan. But, the Bush administration has been shameless in the way they have used the 9/11 terrorist attacks, and the war against terrorism in general, as political tools. The Bush team has exploited the "fear factor" to the fullest extent in recent elections and in establishing flawed government policies. They have used the threat of another terrorist attack on America to frighten voters into reelecting Republicans, to justify creation of a costly and ineffective Department of Homeland Security, to strip away citizens' right to privacy, to justify the unilateral and unnecessary invasion of Iraq, to explain our huge and growing budget deficits, to justify illegal torture and detention of prisoners of war, and to declare unpatriotic anyone who disagrees with the Bush agenda. The war on terrorism has been a cover for all the bad decisions, failed policies, inadequate planning, and overall incompetence of the Bush administration.

The Bush team has seized authority not granted by the Constitution or provided in laws passed by Congress. A compliant Republican Congress allows the Bush regime to narrowly interpret key provisions of some laws dealing with presidential powers and to ignore other laws with which they disagree. President Bush uses a little known instrument, "signing statements," to effectively veto provisions of laws that he opposes. Our president has not vetoed a single bill during his first five years in office, but he has utilized signing statements on more than five hundred occasions. In those signing statements, the president simply defines his interpretations of the laws and how they will be administered. He chooses to ignore key provisions of the laws and adds clarifications that alter the laws so as to reflect what he wants. Nasty battles with Congress over vetoes are thus avoided, and the president interprets the laws in a way that gives him what he desires. One such signing statement was the one President Bush attached to a congressional bill banning torture of prisoners; it enabled him to ignore key provisions of the statute, thus watering down the intended congressional ban on torture of prisoners of war. Congress therefore has no real control over treatment of prisoners, which to me is nothing but raw abuse of presidential power by the Bush administration.

Almost everything the Bush team does is shrouded in secrecy. Policy decisions are made behind closed doors with no input from dissenting voices critical of those policies. The Bush administration refuses to release information detailing who participates in policy discussions, they classify documents simply to prevent their release, and President Bush issued an executive order to block routine release of presidential papers, including those of his father as well as his own. Massive no-bid government contracts are awarded to favored companies without public knowledge and with virtually no oversight. Hundreds of millions of dollars were wasted in the aftermath of Hurricane Katrina, primarily on contracts awarded without competitive bidding. Enormous contracts were handed out to large contractors who, in turn, passed the work down through several levels of subcontractors, with each level raking their profit off the top. Prime contractors for most of the evacuation effort, cleanup work, and rebuilding projects on the Gulf Coast are collecting from two to ten times the amounts the lowest-level subcontractors collect for doing the actual work. The prime contractors and many of the multi-tiered subcontractors are skimming off huge profits for little more than paper work. And, we know who is paying for those lucrative contracts; gullible American taxpayers like you and me foot the bill.

The Bush administration works behind a cover of secrecy in almost all their policy decisions, but what is most troubling is the high level of secrecy surrounding the Bush team's justification to invade Iraq and their execution of that war. Unfavorable prewar intelligence data was suppressed, warnings about a strong post-invasion insurgency were ignored and not made public, requests for greater troop strength were suppressed, illegal detention and torture of prisoners were kept secret, and illegal surveillance of American citizens without warrants was carried out in secret. All of those secret, and mostly illegal, activities were brought to light by journalists, primarily through publishing of leaks of classified information. Now, the Bush administration threatens prosecution and imprisonment of journalists who publish such classified leaks. The Bush team uses distortion, untruths, intimidation, and a shroud of secrecy to hide their flawed policies, failures, and illegal activities.

President Bush has taken the position that he can do what is necessary in time of war, in the name of fighting terrorism. That is a flawed position, a usurping of power not granted to the Office of the President by our Congress or the Constitution. No person in our country is above the law, not even the president. However, a compliant Republican Congress does not have the will or the courage to call President Bush's hand. They have cooperated fully with the Bush administration in all the Republican Party's domestic agenda, and they have supported the president in his rush to war in Iraq and in his botched execution of that war. They know failure of any administration initiative, or any form of censure of the president, will be perceived by the voting public as a failure of the entire Republican Party, hence the Republican Congress continues to support the Bush administration. Our stubborn ideological Executive Branch, together with an equally stubborn and ideological Legislative Branch, have yielded a catastrophic and endless war in Iraq, a gigantic but mostly ineffective

Department of Homeland Security, a domestic agenda heavily tilted toward the wealthy and large corporations, a Medicare prescription drug fiasco, a botched response to Hurricane Katrina, a mountainous national debt to be passed down to our children and grandchildren, and a tarnished national image around the world. Defending that disastrous domestic and foreign policy record has forced the Bush regime to hide behind a larger and larger veil of secrecy; they keep digging a bigger and bigger hole to hide in.

A recent decision by the Bush administration to allow operation of six major U.S. seaports by a company owned by the United Arab Emirates caused an uproar throughout our country. That deal may or may not have posed a security risk, but it was perceived to be a risk by Democrats and Republicans in Congress, as well as by a majority of our citizens. The company purchasing the shipping operations at those six seaports, Dubal Ports World, backed out of the deal, giving President Bush a graceful way out. What we do not know is what kind of pressure was applied to convince Dubal Ports World to renege on the deal, or if anyone in the Bush administration applied that pressure. That opposition to the seaport operations sale is one of the few times the Republican Congress has stood up to the president. Perhaps we have a hopeful sign; maybe Congress will finally exercise some control over an administration that has had a free rein.

The Bush team has never been accused of allowing facts to get in the way of ideology. Intelligence data, scientific analyses, and medical study results have been trumped by ideology and political agenda in the Bush regime. It is common knowledge that President Bush's inner circle of advisors cherry-picked intelligence data on prewar Iraq to justify a decision already made to invade that country. They manipulated intelligence data to convince Congress and the American people that Saddam Hussein possessed weapons of mass destruction and that Iraq was involved with Al Qaeda terrorists in the 9/11 terrorists attack on our country. All those claims proved to be untrue.

The Bush administration has rescinded or relaxed many of the laws and regulations dealing with the environment. They refuse to acknowledge that human-generated greenhouse gasses are contributing to global warming, and they do little or nothing to reduce those gasses. The results of studies performed by National Aeronautics and Space Administration (NASA) scientists concerning pollution and global warming have been filtered and controlled by the Bush team. NASA political appointees routinely alter or restrict news releases and reports that disagree with the Bush administration's policies on environmental issues. Political pressure is also applied to the Food and Drug Administration (FDA) to delay or block release of some drugs, particularly those dealing with contraception or abortion. The FDA, responding to political pressure, concluded more time was needed to research a contraceptive drug, Plan B, although studies had shown the drug was safe for human use without a prescription. That was blatant pandering to the religious right by the Bush administration.

The Bush team and Republican Congress utilize threats and retaliation to discredit and intimidate organizations or individuals who speak out against their flawed policies. For example, a nonprofit organization in Texas, Texans for Public Justice, was critical of campaign spending by Tom DeLay, the former Republican House majority leader and close ally of President Bush. An Internal Revenue Service (IRS) audit of Texans for Public Justice was requested by a close ally of Mr. DeLay, clearly in retaliation for the nonprofit group's criticism of Republican campaign spending. The audit revealed no tax violations by Texans for Public Justice. A well-publicized leak identifying CIA operative Valerie Plame is being investigated by Special Prosecutor Patrick Fitzgerald. A former ambassador, Joseph Wilson, publicly alleged that the Bush team had exaggerated intelligence data to justify invasion of Iraq. A leak by an unnamed administration official identified Mr. Wilson's wife, Valerie Plame, as a CIA operative. Vice President Dick Cheney's chief of staff, Lewis Libby, was indicted in connection with that leak, and he was forced to resign. Mr. Libby is now awaiting trial, and the investigation by Mr. Fitzgerald is continuing.

In their push to gain more power, the Bush administration has shown a disregard for the laws of our land, especially those dealing with presidential powers. Our nation's system of checks and balances has been compromised, partly because of the Republican Congress' reluctance to stand up to President Bush. The resulting lack of accountability has led to more lawlessness and a shroud of secrecy around the Bush team's activities. Such an environment breeds dishonesty, greed for more power, incompetence, and a demand for even greater secrecy.

CHAPTER 8

Media Bias

—⟋⟍—

We are bombarded with news, some of it good, and much of it bad. We read news reports and commentaries in daily newspapers, and we listen to similar newscasts and commentaries on the radio. Radio talk shows are popular, but most of them are extremely biased, spouting out half-truths, innuendos, and outright lies. Television offers a wide variety of news sources. We watch daily newscasts and commentaries, we see live reports of noteworthy news items, we tune in to special newscasts, we view news-related talk shows, we listen to speeches by government officials, we see campaign ads pertaining to political issues or candidates for office, and we watch live debates about various issues and concerns. A large number of our television news sources are reliable and credible, whereas others are not; we must be selective in what we watch. With the advent of the internet, we have ready access to hundreds of legitimate news sites, as well as thousands of unscrupulous web sites and would-be journalists. Millions of "news items" are distributed daily by E-mail, quite often as attachments. Unfortunately, a large percentage of the internet news sources are biased and unreliable. They distort the truth, are misleading, contain blatant lies, and are totally unregulated.

Our various news media perform vital and necessary functions in our society. First and foremost, media outlets keep us informed; they tell us what is happening in our communities and cities, in our states and country, and around the world. We rely on the news media for all kinds of information, most of which we take for granted, and a lot of it we could not do without. A second vital function of the media is to warn us about potential dangers, approaching natural disasters, and other impending health hazards. How else could we prepare for hurricanes, escape from floods, prevent epidemics, and take precautions against a multitude of other health hazards? The media also educates us. News outlets explain current issues to us, tell us where to go for various services and products, give us directions on how to perform many routine tasks, and provide us with other information needed to go about our daily lives. In all those vital functions, we demand honesty, integrity, trustworthiness, and credibility from the news media. We do not want misleading, inaccurate, and biased information in such critical areas.

Who do we rely on to serve as a watchdog over local, state, and federal government agencies? The media, of course. Journalists are the ones who reveal corruption and fraud in government, point out inequalities and bias in our laws and regulations, identify dishonest and crooked government officials and politicians, alert us to waste and mismanagement in government identities, and reveal numerous other improprieties at all levels of government. Do we always demand honesty, accuracy, and bipartisanship when it comes to reporting of such fraud, corruption, waste, bias, and mismanagement in our governments? Sadly, the answer is no. Instead, too many of our citizens want journalists to "overlook" improprieties involving government officials from their own political party, but to come down hard on those officials belonging to the opposing political party. People in

America are reluctant to acknowledge that government officials and politicians within their own political party do indeed make mistakes and commit crimes. That is especially true for staunch supporters of President Bush and the Republican Party. We pay a steep price for the extreme partisanship gripping our country.

Another important role of the news media is that of watchdog over industry. We have discussed at great length the impact on our society of the various industries polluting our water, air, and land. Oil companies, mining operations, timber companies, petrochemical plants, manufacturing companies, land developers, and other similar industries are more concerned about corporate profits than the environment. The Bush administration and Republican Congress, responding to very generous financial support from those polluting industries, have rescinded or relaxed many of the laws and regulations intended to control pollution, and funding has been slashed for government agencies responsible for oversight of those polluting businesses. The task of identifying polluting industries and businesses thus falls on the news media, and they have responded in an admirable fashion. However, faithful Republicans and supporters of the Bush administration do not want to hear truthful news reports about greenhouse gasses and abuse of the environment. They refuse to acknowledge, as does our president, that those polluting industries favored by the Republican Party are contributing to global warming and environmental pollution. They prefer to listen to conservative news outlets and talk shows that echo the Bush administration's position on the environment. Once again, ideology and greed trump truthfulness and reason.

Social conservatives and most staunch Republicans enjoy bashing the "liberal media." But, to them a liberal is anyone who does not support the Bush administration and its flawed policies and does not agree with the religious and moral agenda of the social conservative movement. They have attempted to demonize the Democratic Party, and "liberal" is the nametag they have selected for all Democrats. Republicans go to great extremes in touting their patriotism, a self-proclaimed virtue stemming from their loyal and stubborn support of President Bush and his ill-advised invasion of Iraq. Republicans consider anyone opposed to our president and his unilateral invasion of Iraq to be unpatriotic, and that includes a vast majority of Democrats. So, "unpatriotic liberals" has become the name of choice for Republicans when they refer to Democrats. That broad theme has been incorporated into the messages of conservative news outlets such as Fox News, a mouthpiece for the Bush administration, and radical conservative talk radio. Those far-right news outlets give their loyal base what they want, trashing of "liberal Democrats." Such biased and untruthful media outlets add to the extreme division of our nation.

Does anyone doubt that the Bush administration manipulates the media to suppress unfavorable news reports and promote only news stories that support the president's position? If so, please explain why the American people are never permitted to see flag-draped coffins of our soldiers returning from Iraq. Tell me also why the Bush inner circle so carefully orchestrates our president's personal appearances. Military settings, U.S. soldiers, and the flag are used as backdrops in a majority of his speeches and personal appearances. Extreme measures are taken to prevent any visible demonstrations by those critical of the Bush administration; only loyal supporters are allowed to attend campaign stops, public speeches, and other personal appearances by the president. All questions or comments from the crowds in attendance are carefully screened to ensure that everything said at those appearances is favorable to the president. Any criticism or questioning of the Bush administration and its policies are strictly prohibited. In those rare press conferences when journalists are permitted to question the president, only "friendly" reporters are called upon. President Bush does not want to respond to critical questions or defend his flawed and failed policies in his press conferences.

The Bush administration has taken biased news reporting to a new level. The Office of Global Communications was established in 2003 by executive order as somewhat of a global public relations agency and a clearinghouse for news about Iraq. That office approves, coordinates, and controls messages put out by the Iraq military command, the State Department, and the Pentagon concerning progress of the war in Iraq. It was established to provide rapid responses to criticism of the conduct of the war in Iraq, and it utilizes daily messages of doctored military reports, uncorroborated anecdotes, and propaganda to paint a rosy picture of the conflict's progress. Journalists embedded in military units in Iraq operate under strict guidelines, and any reporter who questions or criticizes the conduct of the war runs the risk of being labeled unpatriotic by the Bush team.

Another disgraceful practice of the Bush administration is to "buy" pro-American and Pro-Bush opinion articles in Iraqi newspapers and on Iraqi television, as well as in news outlets in our country. The administration gives large grants to conservative multimedia conglomerates for pushing the president's policies in television shows, radio broadcasts, and newspaper articles. Conservative pundits have also received payments from lobbyist Jack Abramoff, who recently pleaded guilty to bribery charges, for publishing articles favorable to Republican causes. Those conservative journalists did not necessarily disagree with the opinion pieces they published, but they probably would not have written them except for the payments they received. These are examples of how the Bush administration and Republican lobbyists control and manipulate the media. And, it will continue as long as American citizens sit back and refuse to challenge such excesses. A free press, an unbiased media, is necessary for a true democracy. A state-controlled media leads to a totalitarian system of government, one that does not allow the individual freedoms we have in our nation.

America desperately needs honest and trustworthy news reporters and journalists, someone to tell us about all the bad things happening in our country. Without a free and unbiased media, who will inform us about corruption in government, corporate greed, environmental abuses, deficiencies in our healthcare system, irregularities in elections, deficiencies in our schools, overcrowding in our prisons, high incidences of divorce and teenage pregnancies, inequalities in our tax system, civil rights abuses, unfair labor practices, and a myriad of other problems plaguing our society. How can a true patriot tolerate manipulation and control of our media by our government, simply for political gain? Each one of us should consume news from several sources, including those with which we disagree, and demand accurate and unbiased reporting from our news media. That would help reduce the extreme polarization in our nation.

The various media outlets provide us with all kinds of news and information, some biased and some unbiased, but how do we receive and respond to that news and information? Quite a few of our citizens are uninformed; they reject news reports, or they ignore them. Those people are unconcerned about key issues in our society, and they have little or no knowledge pertaining to the issues. A second category of citizens are misinformed; they consume only biased news and information, and they reject any view other than their own. Those misinformed people are usually deeply concerned about the issues, but their knowledge about the issues is biased and somewhat limited. Those misinformed citizens listen to only one side of any debate about controversial issues; they have a closed mind. A large number of far-right conservatives and many social conservatives fit into the misinformed mold. They listen only to conservative news outlets and talk shows, so much of the news and information they receive is biased, misleading, or inaccurate.

A third segment of our population consists of informed citizens, those people who consume news and information from various media outlets, both biased and unbiased. That group is very concerned about key issues, they are willing to listen to both sides of the debates about those issues, they are open-minded, and they have developed a broad understanding of the issues. Obviously, our country would be better off if all our citizens were included in the informed segment of our population, but that is not the case. Too many Americans are either uninformed or misinformed about the important issues facing our nation. That critical lack of knowledge contributes to the extreme polarization of our country.

Let us pause now and do a reality check. Do you fit into the informed, misinformed, or uninformed segment of our population? Let us understand, though, that all of us have certain issues about which we have a closed mind; we reject any view other than our own with regard to those issues. That means we are all misinformed to some extent. A few key questions, together with your honest answers to them, will help determine which category of citizens you belong to. Financial analysts predict that, without some changes, our social security system will not be able to pay retirees their full benefits by about year 2040. The first question is, "Will President Bush's proposed private accounts for social security extend that shortfall deadline to a later date?" Implementation of the Bush plan for privatized social security accounts, with no other changes, would result in a shortfall much sooner than year 2040. So, if you answered "yes" to that question, you are misinformed. The second question is, "Did Saddam Hussein possess weapons of mass destruction when we invaded Iraq?" Inspectors have verified that Iraq had no weapons of mass destruction or ongoing programs to develop biological weapons, chemical weapons, or nuclear arms. Again, a "yes" answer to that second question indicates you are misinformed. The third key question is, "Was Saddam Hussein involved with the Al Qaeda terrorists in the 9/11 terrorists attack on our country?" The recently released 9/11 Commission Report proved Iraq was not involved in the 9/11 terrorists attack on America, so once again, a "yes" answer to that question means you are misinformed.

Anyone who answered yes to any of those three key questions should do some serious soul-searching and consider turning to different news sources; their current sources of news and information are biased, misleading, and inaccurate. Faithfully trusting in everything the Bush administration tells us, stubbornly supporting some of the flawed Republican Party policies and corrupt politicians, and dogmatically following the narrow social conservative agenda increase the partisan division in our nation. A true democracy is characterized by compromise and give-and-take in government, and the majority in control does not force its will on the minority. America is drifting farther and farther away from a true democracy; we are sliding toward a dictatorship. America, we must wake up and put a stop to the actions that lead to such extreme polarization of our population.

CHAPTER 9

An Overview of the Polarization in Our Country

—ⱳ—

We have studied in great depth the extreme division that grips our nation. Americans cannot agree on either the issues that have spawned that polarization, just who is responsible for the partisanship, or what measures we should implement to alleviate some of the bickering and strife. We have considered the sharp differences of opinion amongst our citizens on religious and moral issues, especially those hot-button issues at the forefront of the social conservative movement. Also examined was the pronounced political division in our country, a division that divides our population almost evenly. That intense political strife is primarily between the Republican Party and the Democratic Party, but it encroaches on virtually every aspect of our society. That strife is fueled to a large extent by the Republican Party agenda and the ideology of its leadership.

The sharp political division in our nation is most evident in the class warfare we see all around us. It is essentially a struggle between the wealthy and the poor, between big business and the working class. The Republican Party has always favored large corporations and wealthy people, but that bias is becoming more and more pronounced. Enormous tax cuts and tax subsidies passed by a Republican Congress were structured to benefit wealthy citizens and big business, to the detriment of everyone else. Republican-backed tort reform laws are tilted heavily in favor of big business and against consumers. And, recently-passed bankruptcy legislation makes it much more difficult for consumers to declare bankruptcy, thus increasing the profits of credit card companies and other financial institutions. The Bush administration and Republican Congress have slashed funding for welfare programs, Medicaid, veterans' benefits, student loans, and virtually all of the other social programs. Environmental laws and regulations have been rescinded or relaxed by a Republican administration to boost profits of oil companies, timber companies, petrochemical plants, mining operations, and other polluting industries. Civil rights laws and regulations have been watered down by a Republican Congress and the Bush administration to roll back some fifty years of civil rights progress in our country. This list of perks for the rich goes on and on.

The extreme partisanship of our population can be attributed to a variety of sources, but I believe five major factors have been responsible for a lion's share of the division we see in America. First, I believe, is the negative impact of the fundamentalism inherent in the social conservative movement. Christian social conservatives are committed to very narrow and strongly-held religious and moral views. They are opposed to abortion and euthanasia, they favor prayer in public schools, they are against any form of gay marriage and homosexuality, and they want creationism to be taught in our public schools' science classes. All of these issues are of utmost importance to social conservatives, and they refuse to tolerate any view other than their own. These folks are outspoken in their beliefs, they are committed to getting their religious and moral agenda incorporated into our nation's laws and government policies, and they are heavily involved at all levels of our political system. The political influence of social conservatives is considerably greater than their numbers would indicate. Needless to say, the fundamentalist attitude and actions of social conservatives lead to animosity and division throughout our society.

The political ideology of the Republican Party, and particularly that of the Bush administration, is also a major source of polarization in our country. Social conservatives have been warmly embraced by the Republican Party, and the religious and moral agenda of the social conservative movement has been incorporated into the Republican Party platform. As a result, it is difficult to differentiate between the fundamentalism of social conservatives and the ideology of the Republican Party. Both faithful Republicans and social conservatives are passionate about the issues, actively involved in the political process, consistent voters, and intolerant of any belief other than their own. Social conservatives and right-wing Republicans believe almost any action, legal or not, is justified if it furthers their cause. That includes demonizing the opposition by means of misrepresentations, half-truths, innuendos, and outright falsehoods. Social conservatives and Republicans frame the debates on issues as struggles between good and evil, with them always being on the side of good. That mind set obviously leads to polarization of our population.

A third major factor is the impact of big money in politics. The costs of political campaigns have increased dramatically over the last twenty or so years, primarily because of the tremendous impact of television on the political landscape. Politicians and political parties rely on major financial supporters and political action committees (PACs) for the funds necessary to mount effective campaigns. As a result, our elected officials and political parties are beholden to those big-money interests when it comes time to pass legislation. They pass laws and regulations favorable to the large corporations and rich folks who contribute the big bucks to their campaigns. In other words, PACs, large corporations, and wealthy individuals have "bought" many of our elected officials and other government people. That is especially true for the Republican Party which has always been biased toward big business and well-heeled folks. Those special-interest groups demand legislation and regulations favorable to them, but detrimental to poor people, consumers, and the working class. Powerless citizens hurt the most by the Republican Party policies are primarily Democrats and others who do not exercise their right to vote, so those people are of no concern to the Republican Party and the special-interest groups who foot the bill for their reelections. Such control of our government by monied special-interest groups does breed animosity and division within our nation.

The Bush administration's decision to invade Iraq, together with a severe lack of planning to control the postwar insurgency, added to the partisanship already in America. A large number of our citizens were against the unilateral invasion of Iraq, and they resent the way the Bush inner circle manipulated intelligence data to justify the war. Those people also realized that such an invasion of a sovereign Arab country would most likely increase terrorism, not eliminate it as the Bush administration claimed. The whole Iraq conflict and postwar reconstruction efforts have been bungled by the Bush administration, but they refuse to admit any mistakes or to acknowledge the war in Iraq is not going well. To add insult to injury, President Bush and his faithful supporters have labeled anyone opposed to the Iraq invasion as being unpatriotic. They even stooped so low as to call decorated and severely wounded war veterans fakes and cowards. That holier-than-thou questioning of American citizens' patriotism has been one of the most polarizing aspects of the entire Iraq fiasco.

From the time he was "appointed" president by a conservative-leaning Supreme Court, after a close and controversial election, President Bush and his inner circle have worked to consolidate and increase presidential power. They have refused to heed dissenting voices, their decisions and actions have been shrouded in secrecy, they have coerced and intimidated a Republican Congress to support their extreme ideological agenda, they have manipulated and controlled the news media, they have not been truthful with the American people, they have quietly dismantled or under-funded federal agencies which have oversight responsibilities, they have misused the Department of Homeland Security to enhance presidential power, and they have illegally used our nation's intelligence agencies for political purposes. The Bush team is leading our country away from a true democracy toward a totalitarian form of government, one that is not consistent with our Constitution and Bill of Rights. All those actions by a power-driven and ideological administration have added to the partisanship in our country.

The Republican Party, supported and guided by social conservatives, is striving to incorporate the religious and moral agenda of the social conservative movement into our laws and government policies. For all practical purposes, social conservatives cannot be separated from the Republican Party; they function as one political identity. They frame debates on critical issues as good versus evil, and they claim to be on the side of good. These right-wingers utilize very narrow interpretations of the Bible to support their views on controversial issues, and they claim God is on their side. Social conservatives cite Scripture as the basis of their religious, moral, and social agenda, thus implying that anyone opposed to their views is not obeying the Bible and its teaching. Also, Republicans claim to be a family-values party and perceive themselves as being compassionate conservatives. The remainder of this book is devoted primarily to determining if all those claims by social conservatives and Republicans are valid. Numerous Scripture passages are examined to determine if the social conservative movement does indeed incorporate pure religion (grounded in the Bible) or if hypocrisy is its foundation.

The Bible, God's Word, contains a multitude of commandments, instructions, and examples telling us how we should live our lives, all of which are valid guidelines for us. We refer to the Scriptures as our roadmap of life, but how do we apply the Bible's teaching to our society in year 2006? How do we choose Biblical guidelines relevant to issues we face in America today, and how do we condense the hundreds of commandments and instructions into a manageable number that relate directly to those issues? We first review key Scripture passages in the Old Testament to find out what God expected from His chosen people, the Israelites (or Jews), prior to the birth of His Son, Jesus Christ. We then consider pertinent Bible passages from the New Testament to determine what God desires from Christians, His people today. Our primary goal is to determine if the social conservative agenda and Republican Party policies are consistent with the overall teaching of the Bible. We do not want to get bogged down in the details; instead, we want to focus on the overriding theme and message of the Scriptures. We must keep an open mind as we study relevant Bible passages if we hope to gain a better understanding of how God's Word relates to our society in year 2006.

CHAPTER 10

Pure Religion in the Old Testament

—⁄⁄⁄—

God's chosen people in the Old Testament were the children of Israel, or the nation Israel, often referred to as God's covenant people. Abraham (or Abram) is considered to be the Father of Israel, and God's call of Abraham to that role is presented in the Book of Genesis in the Bible.

> Terah took his son Abram, his grandson Lot son of Haran, and his daughter-in-law Sarai, the wife of his son Abram, and together they set out from Ur of the Chaldeans to go to Canaan. But when they came to Haran, they settled there.
> —Genesis 11:31 NIV

The Lord had said to Abram, "Leave your country, your people and your father's household and go to the land I will show you. "I will make you into a great nation and I will bless you; I will make your name great, and you will be a blessing. I will bless those who bless you, and whoever curses you I will curse; and all peoples on earth will be blessed through you." So Abram left, as the Lord had told him; and Lot went with him. Abram was seventy-five years old when he set out from Haran. He took his wife Sarai, his nephew Lot, all the possessions they had accumulated and the people they had acquired in Haran, and they set out for the land of Canaan, and they arrived there.

—Genesis 12:1-5 NIV

Abram obeyed God's call. He left Haran, taking his family and possessions, and set out for the land of Canaan, not knowing just where God would lead him. God established a covenant with Abraham, and later confirmed that covenant with Abraham's son, Isaac, and his grandson, Jacob.

Then the word of the Lord came to him: "This man will not be your heir, but a son coming from your own body will be your heir." He took him outside and said, "Look up at the heavens and count the stars—if indeed you can count them." Then he said to him, "So shall your offspring be." Abram believed the Lord, and he credited it to him as righteousness....On that day the Lord made a covenant with Abram and said, "To your descendants I give this land, from the river of Egypt to the great river, the Euphrates—".... —Genesis 15:4-6,18 NIV

The Lord appeared to Isaac and said, "Do not go down to Egypt; live in the land where I tell you to live. Stay in this land for a while, and I will be with you and will bless you. For to you and your descendants I will give all these lands and will confirm the oath I swore to your father Abraham. I will make your descendants as numerous as the stars in the sky and will give them all these lands, and through your offspring all nations on earth will be blessed, because Abraham obeyed me

and kept my requirements, my commands, my decrees and my laws."
—Genesis 26:2-5 NIV

There above it stood the Lord, and he said: "I am the Lord, the God of your father Abraham and the God of Isaac. I will give you and your descendants the land on which you are lying. Your descendants will be like the dust of the earth, and you will spread out to the west and to the east, to the north and to the south. All peoples on earth will be blessed through you and your offspring. I am with you and will watch over you wherever you go, and I will bring you back to this land. I will not leave you until I have done what I have promised you."
—Genesis 28:13-15 NIV

God was true to His promise. Over some four hundred years while in Egyptian bondage, Jacob's twelve sons multiplied, with Abraham's descendants then numbering over 600,000 men, plus the women and children.

God called Moses to lead His chosen people out of bondage in Egypt, back to the land of Canaan, their Promised Land. That exodus from Egypt to Canaan consumed forty years, during which time God gave Moses a code of laws in order to reveal His will with respect to the Israelites' conduct in Canaan. We refer to that code of laws for Israel as the Mosaic Law, which includes the Ten Commandments. Occasionally, reference to the Law means only the Ten Commandments, but generally it includes all the divinely instituted commands and precepts mediated through Moses to govern the overall conduct of God's people. The entire Mosaic Law is included in the first five books of the Old Testament, from Genesis through Deuteronomy. Very detailed instructions are given with regard to worship practices, sacrifices and offerings, special feasts, observance of the Sabbath, dietary restrictions, family responsibilities, tithing, financial responsibilities, sexual considerations, laws and courts, punishment for sin, and every other aspect of conduct.

Obviously, such a demanding and complex set of rules and regulations is virtually impossible to follow, so what did God really expect from His people? The remaining books in the Old Testament show us how God dealt with His people Israel. We see a repetitive cycle of Israel turning from their one true God to pagan gods, their practicing a lifestyle of sin and immorality, God's disciplining and judgment of Israel for their sins, the people's repentance for their sins, and God's forgiveness and restoration of the Israelites to their status as God's people. What exactly were the sins of Israel that brought on God's judgment? The historical and prophetic books of the Old Testament, from Joshua through Malachi, cover a multitude of sins and wrongdoing committed by the people of Israel, but I believe we can condense them down into three major categories.

Before we consider those three sin categories, however, it is worthwhile for us to review the Ten Commandments. Those basic commandments are the foundation for all the detailed instructions and precepts incorporated into the overall Mosaic Law, as well as a code of conduct for people today.

And God spoke all these words: "I am the Lord your God, who brought you out of Egypt, out of the land of slavery. "You shall have no other gods before me. "You shall not make yourself an idol in the form of anything in heaven above or on the earth beneath or in the waters below. You shall not bow down to them or worship them; for I, the Lord your God, am a jealous God, punishing the children for the sin of the fathers to the third and fourth generation of those who hate me, but showing love to a thousand generations of those who love me and keep my commandments. "You shall not misuse the name of the Lord your God, for the Lord will not hold anyone guiltless who misuses his name. "Remember the Sabbath day by keeping it holy. Six days you shall labor and do all your work, but the seventh day is a Sabbath to the Lord your God. On it you shall not do any work, neither you, nor your son or daughter, nor your manservant or maidservant, nor your animals, nor the alien within your gates. For in six days the Lord made the heavens and the earth, the sea, and all that is in them, but he rested on the seventh day. Therefore the Lord blessed the Sabbath day and made it holy. "Honor your father and your mother, so that you may live long in the land the Lord your God is giving you. "You shall not murder. "You shall not commit adultery. "You shall not steal. "You shall not give false testimony against your neighbor. "You shall not covet your neighbor's house. You shall not covet your neighbor's wife, or his manservant or maidservant, his ox or donkey, or anything that belongs to your neighbor."

—Exodus 20:1-17 NIV

The first four commandments deal with the Israelites, and our, relationship with God, and they are of utmost importance. We cannot hope to obey the remaining commandments if we do not have a right relationship with the Lord. The last six commandments focus on our relationships with others, starting with our fathers and mothers. So, let us not forget that the sins of the Israelites, as well as our sins, are the result of either a wrong relationship with God or wrong relationships with one another.

The most significant and the most prevalent sin committed by the people of Israel was that of turning away from God and His ways and turning to false pagan gods. Israel's turning away from the Lord, and thus disobedience of His laws and precepts, is the main theme of the prophets' messages to the people of Israel. The primary responsibility of the prophets was to deliver God's messages to His people, but quite often those messages were not what the people wanted to hear. The Book of Judges contains numerous accounts of the Israelites turning from the Lord to pagan deities, God's judgment on them, their repentance, and God's deliverance and restoration.

The Israelites did evil in the eyes of the Lord; they forgot the Lord their God and served the Baals and the Asherahs. The anger of the Lord burned against Israel so that he sold them into the hands of Cushan-Rishathaim king of Aram Naharaim, to whom the Israelites were subject for eight years. But when they cried out to the Lord, he raised up for them a deliverer, Othniel son of Kenaz, Caleb's younger brother, who saved them. The spirit of the Lord came upon him, so that he became Israel's judge and went to war. The Lord gave Cushan-Rishathaim king of

Aram into the hands of Othniel, who overpowered him. So the land had peace for forty years, until Othniel son of Kenaz died.

—Judges 3:7-11 NIV

Once again the Israelites did evil in the eyes of the Lord, and because they did this evil the Lord gave Eglon king of Moab power over Israel. Getting the Ammonites and Amalekites to join him, Eglon came and attacked Israel, and they took possession of the City of Palms. The Israelites were subject to Eglon king of Moab for eighteen years. Again the Israelites cried out to the Lord, and he gave them a deliverer—Ehud, a left-handed man, the son of Gera the Benjamite. The Israelites sent him with tribute to Eglon king of Moab...."Follow me," he ordered, "for the Lord has given Moab, your enemy, into your hands." So they followed him down and, taking possession of the fords of the Jordan that led to Moab, they allowed no one to cross over. At that time they struck down about ten thousand Moabites, all vigorous and strong; not a man escaped. That day Moab was made subject to Israel, and the land had peace for eighty years.

—Judges 3:12-15, 28-30 NIV

These two episodes in Israel's history are typical examples of how God, or the Lord, dealt with His people. The Israelites would enjoy a period of peace and prosperity, but they would turn away from God and start serving the pagan gods in their midst. The Lord would then allow a pagan nation to conquer Israel, and they would be under the dominion of that pagan nation for a number of years. The people would finally repent and cry out to the Lord, and He would raise up a deliverer to lead them out of bondage. Israel would have peace and prosperity for another long time period, and the cycle would be repeated.

The prophetic books of the Old Testament include similar accounts of Israel, or Judah, turning away from the Lord and turning to the worship of pagan gods or idols. Some of the prophets lived during the time when the twelve tribes of Israel were joined as the United Kingdom of Israel, whereas others lived after the twelve tribes of Israel were split into the Divided Kingdoms of Israel and Judah.

> I will pronounce my judgments on my people because of their wickedness in forsaking me, in burning incense to other gods and in worshiping what their hands have made.
> —Jeremiah 1:16 NIV

Hear the word of the Lord, O house of Jacob, all you clans of the house of Israel. This is what the Lord says: "What fault did your fathers find in me, that they strayed so far from me? They followed worthless idols and became worthless themselves. They did not ask, 'Where is the Lord, who brought us up out of Egypt and led us through the barren wilderness, through a land of deserts and rifts, a land of drought and darkness, a land where no one travels and no one lives?' I brought you into a fertile land to eat its fruit and rich produce. But you came and defiled my land and made my inheritance detestable. The priests did not ask, 'Where is the Lord?' Those who deal with the law did not know me; the leaders rebelled against me. The prophets prophesied by Baal, following worthless idols."

—Jeremiah 2:4-8 NIV

These passages in the Book of Jeremiah give an account of Israel's long history of unfaithfulness. The Israelites repeatedly strayed from the Lord, the One who had delivered them from bondage in Egypt and to the Promised Land of Canaan. The religious leaders and experts in the Law rebelled against God to serve pagan gods and idols. Through Jeremiah, the Lord pleaded with His people to return to Him, and God offered Israel forgiveness and restoration if they would only repent.

Ezekiel, a prophet in Judah, delivered messages of God's judgment on the nation of Judah and its capital city, Jerusalem. His messages from the Lord came in the form of visions, and they came before the fall of Jerusalem to the Babylonians. One such vision came to Ezekiel when he was at his home, and it came in the presence of some elders (leaders of Judah). Ezekiel was in exile in Babylonia at the time of that vision.

In the sixth year, in the sixth month on the fifth day, while I was sitting in my house and the elders of Judah were sitting before me, the hand of the Sovereign Lord came upon me there.
—Ezekiel 8:1 NIV

Then he said to me, "Son of man, look toward the north." So I looked, and in the entrance north of the gate of the altar I saw this idol of jealousy. And he said to me, "Son of man, do you see what they are doing—the utterly detestable things the house of Israel is doing here, things that will drive me far from my sanctuary? But you will see things that are even more detestable."
—Ezekiel 8:5-6 NIV

And he said to me, "Go in and see the wicked and detestable things they are doing here." So I went in and looked, and I saw portrayed all over the walls all kinds of crawling things and detestable animals and all the idols of the house of Israel. In front of them stood seventy elders of the house of Israel, and Jaazaniah son of Shaphan was standing among them. Each had a censer in his hand, and a fragrant cloud of incense was rising. He said to me, "Son of man, have you seen what the elders of the house of Israel are doing in the darkness, each at the shrine of his own idol? They say, 'The Lord does not see us; the Lord has forsaken the land.'" Again, he said, "You will see them doing things that are even more detestable."

—Ezekiel 8:9-13 NIV

Then he brought me to the entrance of the north gate of the house of the Lord, and I saw women sitting there, mourning for Tammuz. He said to me, "Do you see this, son of man? You will see things that are even more detestable than this."

—Ezekiel 8:14-15 NIV

He then brought me into the inner court of the house of the Lord, and there at the entrance to the temple, between the portico and the altar, were about twenty-five men. With their backs toward the temple of the Lord and their faces toward the

east, they were bowing down to the sun in the east. He said to me, "Have you seen this, son of man? Is it a trivial matter for the house of Judah to do the detestable things they are doing here? Must they also fill the land with violence and continually provoke me to anger? Look at them putting the branch to their nose! Therefore I will deal with them in anger; I will not look on them with pity or spare them. Although they shout in my ears, I will not listen to them."
—Ezekiel 8:16-18

Ezekiel gave the exact time and place of this vision. He was at home while in exile in Babylonia when leaders from the other Judah exiles came to visit him. This particular vision focuses on the abhorrent worship practices in the temple back in Jerusalem. Verses 5-6 describe worship of a pagan god, the "idol of jealousy," inside the temple at the altar gate. That idol located near the altar provoked the Lord to jealousy; He did not want His people to be drawn to any other god. This form of jealousy is considered to be a positive attribute. Verses 9-13 depict animal worship inside the temple. The elders were burning incense and worshiping images of animals painted on the walls of a hidden area in the temple. The elders knew such worship of animals was forbidden by the Lord, but they believed He could not see them. Verses 14-15 portray women in the temple area worshiping Tammuz, a Babylonian fertility god. By worshiping that pagan fertility god, the women were expressing their belief that Tammuz, rather than the Lord, would bring fertility to their land. We see in verses 16-18 sun worship in the temple, probably by priests. Sun worship was a common practice in the ancient pagan world, but the Israelites were forbidden to worship any thing or anyone other than their true God.

There are many other accounts in the Old Testament of the Israelites turning from Jehovah God to the pagan deities in their midst. Turning from the Lord to pagan deities did not necessarily mean the Israelites had stopped worshiping Jehovah God. Quite often, they worshiped both the Lord and pagan gods, so they still considered themselves to be God's people. What they did not realize, however, was that they could not do both; God demands his people's total allegiance. Their shared worship of the Lord, along with pagan deities, was thus superficial and insincere, and it was totally unacceptable to God.

The Israelites' turning away from the Lord to pagan gods led to the second major category of sins, that of immorality and wicked living. The people of Israel took on the lifestyles and cultures of the pagan societies whose gods they worshiped. They were guilty of adultery, murder, cheating, lying, and all kinds of wickedness. The prophet Hosea's marriage to his unfaithful wife, Gomer, symbolized the relationship between the Lord and His unfaithful people, Israel. Gomer's marriage infidelity was analogous to Israel's spiritual infidelity.

Hear the word of the Lord, you Israelites, because the Lord has a charge to bring against you who live in the land: "There is no faithfulness, no love, no acknowledgment of God in the land. There is only cursing, lying and murder, stealing and adultery; they break all bounds, and bloodshed follows bloodshed. Because of this the land mourns, and all who live in it waste away; the

beasts of the field and the birds of the air and the
fish of the sea are dying."
—Hosea 4:1-3 NIV

Through Hosea, the Lord charged Israel with turning
away from Him, and He charged them with all kinds of
sinful living. Verse 2 portrays Israel as a nation characterized by a complete breakdown of morality. Even
nature was affected by the sins of the people. The land,
the animals, the birds, and the fish were adversely
affected by Israel's sins.

"You stumble day and night, and the prophets
stumble with you. So I will destroy your mother—
my people are destroyed from lack of knowledge. "Because you have rejected knowledge, I
also reject you as my priests; because you have
ignored the law of your God, I also will ignore
your children. The more the priests increased,
the more they sinned against me; they exchanged
their Glory for something disgraceful. They feed
on the sins of my people and relish their wickedness. And it will be: Like people, like priests. I

will punish both of them for their ways and repay
them for their deeds."
—Hosea 4:5-9 NIV

The priests were responsible for instructing the people
in matters of the Law, but they had failed to do so. The
priests were just as guilty as the people, so God's judgment would come down on both the people and the religious leaders.

Another vision by the prophet Ezekiel indicates
the wide range of sins committed by the Israelites in
Jerusalem. Those detestable sins by the people were the
result of their turning from God to the pagan deities all
around them.

> The word of the Lord came to me: "Son of man,
> will you judge her? Will you judge this city of
> bloodshed? Then confront her with all her detest-
> able practices and say: 'This is what the Sovereign
> Lord says: O city that brings on herself doom by
> shedding blood in her midst and defiles herself by
> making idols, you have become guilty because of
> the blood you have shed and have become defiled

by the idols you have made. You have brought your days to a close, and the end of your years has come. Therefore I will make you an object of scorn to the nations and a laughingstock to all the countries.....'"See how each of the princes of Israel who are in you uses his power to shed blood. In you they have treated father and mother with contempt; in you they have oppressed the alien and mistreated the fatherless and the widow. You have despised my holy things and desecrated my Sabbaths. In you are slanderous men bent on shedding blood; in you are those who eat at the mountain shrines and commit lewd acts. In you are those who dishonor their fathers' bed; in you are those who violate women during their period, when they are ceremonially unclean. In you one man commits a detestable offense with his neighbor's wife, another shamefully defiles his daughter-in-law, and another violates his sister, his own father's daughter. In you men accept bribes to shed blood; you take usury and excessive interest and make unjust gain from your

neighbors by extortion. And you have forgotten me, declares the Sovereign Lord.'"
—Ezekiel 22: 1-4,6-12 NIV

The inhabitants of Jerusalem worshiped idols in pagan shrines, shed innocent blood, treated their parents with contempt, committed all kinds of immoral sexual acts, did not observe the Sabbath, cheated their neighbors, and forgot the Lord. The preceding passage in Ezekiel is only one of numerous times the Bible addresses the sins of Israel and Judah.

The Lord saw how great man's wickedness on the earth had become, and that every inclination of the thoughts of his heart was only evil all the time. The Lord was grieved that he had made man on the earth, and his heart was filled with pain. So the Lord said, "I will wipe mankind, whom I have created, from the face of the earth—men and animals, and creatures that move along the ground, and birds of the air—for I am grieved that I made them." But Noah found favor in the eyes of the Lord.....Now the earth was corrupt

in God's sight and was full of violence. God
saw how corrupt the earth had become, for all
the people on earth had corrupted their ways. So
God said to Noah, "I am going to put an end to
all people, for the earth is filled with violence
because of them. I am surely going to destroy
both them and the earth."
—Genesis 6:5-8,11-13 NIV

"Why should I forgive you? Your children have
forsaken me and sworn by gods that are not gods.
I supplied all their needs, yet they committed
adultery and thronged to the houses of prostitutes. They are well-fed, lusty stallions, each
neighing for another man's wife."
—Jeremiah 5:7-8 NIV

But your inequities have separated you from
your God; your sins have hidden his face from
you, so that he will not hear. For your hands are
stained with blood, your fingers with guilt. Your
lips have spoken lies, and your tongue mutters
wicked things. No one calls for justice; no one

pleads his case with integrity. They rely on empty arguments and speak lies; they conceive trouble and give birth to evil.....Their deeds are evil deeds, and acts of violence are in their hands. Their feet rush into sin; they are swift to shed innocent blood. Their thoughts are evil thoughts; ruin and destruction mark their ways. The way of peace they do not know; there is no justice in their paths. They have turned them into crooked roads; no one who walks in them will know peace.

—Isaiah 59:2-4,6b-8 NIV

Judah did evil in the eyes of the Lord. By the sins they committed they stirred up his jealous anger more than their fathers had done. They also set up for themselves high places, sacred stones and Asherah poles on every high hill and under every spreading tree. There were even male shrine prostitutes in the land; the people engaged in all the detestable practices of the nations the Lord had driven out before the Israelites.

—1 Kings 14:22-24 NIV

Nadab son of Jeroboam became king of Israel in the second year of Asa king of Judah, and he reigned over Israel two years. He did evil in the eyes of the Lord, walking in the ways of his father and in his sin, which he had caused Israel to commit.

— 1 Kings 15:25-26

In the third year of Asa king of Judah, Baasha son of Ahijah became king of all Israel in Tirzah, and he reigned twenty-four years. He did evil in the eyes of the Lord, walking in the ways of Jeroboam and in his sin, which he caused Israel to commit.

— 1 Kings 15:33-34

From the time of Noah, when the Lord sent a great flood on the earth, people have lived sinful and corrupt lives. The historical books of the Bible and the prophets paint the picture of a rebellious people who turn from the one true God to worship false gods. They commit detestable sins of all kinds, including sins of immorality. God demands total allegiance from His people, and He hates sin, so such corrupt and sinful conduct brings on God's judgment.

The third major category of sins committed by the Israelites involved their treatment of the poor, weak, and helpless in their society. Mistreatment of the down-trodden is addressed by the prophets in numerous Scripture passages, second in number only to the Bible passages charging the Israelites with turning from the Lord to pagan gods. Those sins against the poor and powerless include a legal system partial to the wealthy, oppression of the poor and helpless, defrauding poor people out of their homes and inheritances, bribery and extortion, dishonesty in the marketplace, cheating employees out of their wages, forcing people into slavery, and false teaching by the religious leaders. Throughout the Bible, God is a champion of those who cannot help themselves, and the Scriptures come down hard on those who abuse, neglect, or mistreat the poor and helpless among us.

The Mosaic Law defines in great detail how the Israelites were to treat one another, and the prophets charged the people of Israel with violating those laws and precepts. Let us consider just a few of the many

Scripture passages addressing that critical aspect of the Israelites' conduct.

Learn to do right! Seek justice, encourage the oppressed. Defend the cause of the fatherless, plead the case of the widow.
—Isaiah 1:17 NIV

"'Do not pervert justice; do not show partiality to the poor or favoritism to the great, but judge your neighbor fairly.'"
—Leviticus 19:15 NIV

The Lord works righteousness and justice for all the oppressed. He made known his ways to Moses, his deeds to the people of Israel:....
—Psalm 103:6-7 NIV

"Because of the oppression of the weak and the groaning of the needy, I will now arise," says the Lord. "I will protect them from those who malign them."
—Psalm 12:5 NIV

Selfishness and self-centeredness have characterized the human race since the first sin of Adam and Eve in the Garden of Eden. All human beings are born with a nature and an environment inclined to sin; all of us have sinned. The wealthy and strong have oppressed and mistreated the poor and weak throughout the history of humankind. In the Scripture passages in Isaiah, Leviticus, and Psalms, the Bible informs us such behavior is in violation of God's laws and instructions to the people of Israel, and to us as well.

Prophets from Isaiah and Joel to Malachi charged the people of Israel and Judah with disobedience and perversion of God's commandments and precepts. They called for repentance by the people and proclaimed God's judgment on those who did not turn back to the Lord and His ways.

Woe to those who make unjust laws, to those who issue oppressive decrees, to deprive the poor of their rights and withhold justice from the oppressed of my people, making widows their prey and robbing the fatherless.
—Isaiah 10:1-2 NIV

The oracle that Habakkuk the prophet received. How long, O Lord, must I call for help, but you do not listen? Or cry out to you, "Violence!" but you do not save? Why do you make me look at injustice? Why do you tolerate wrong? Destruction and violence are before me; there is strife, and conflict abounds. Therefore the law is paralyzed, and justice never prevails. The wicked hem in the righteous, so that justice is perverted.

—Habakkuk 1:1-4 NIV

Woe to those who plan inequity, to those who plot evil on their beds! At morning's light they carry it out because it is in their power to do it. They covet fields and seize them, and houses, and take them. They defraud a man of his home, a fellowman of his inheritance.

—Micah 2:1-2 NIV

You hate the one who reproves in court and despise him who tells the truth. You trample on the poor and force him to give you grain. Therefore, though you have built stone mansions, you will not live in them; though you have planted lush vineyards, you will not drink their wine. For I know how many are your offenses and how great your sins. You oppress the righteous and take bribes and you deprive the poor of justice in the courts.

—Amos 5:10-12 NIV

These Scripture passages are addressed primarily to those who pervert the law and the courts to cheat and oppress the poor and helpless. The charges enumerated are against the rulers, religious leaders, judges, and other powerful and wealthy people. In Biblical times, widows, orphans, and aliens represented needy and helpless people. They could not own property, and they had very little means of support. The poor and weak were those people who owned very limited material possessions, barely eked out a living, and were unable to defend themselves in the legal system. They were at the mercy of the rulers, judges, wealthy people, and religious leaders.

Those in power in Israel and Judah were guilty of establishing unjust laws and decrees, laws that would benefit themselves and penalize the poor and helpless in their society. The powerful and well connected plotted to cheat poor people out of their fields, homes, and inheritances. That was accomplished in a legal system wherein untruthful testimony was heard and tolerated, unjust laws were enforced, and judges were bribed. Extortion was utilized to obtain the meager possessions of poor people, and violence was quite often employed by those in power. The widows, orphans, and other helpless people were denied any means of help and support. The rulers, judges, and wealthy people used the spoils of their unlawful and dishonest activities to maintain their high standard of living.

The people of Israel and Judah practiced slavery. Oftentimes, a person became a slave when he or she was captured in warfare; the victor in war took those who were conquered as slaves. Poor Israelites also became slaves as payment for debts they could not pay. Poor families even sold their children into slavery as payment of debts they owed.

This is what the Lord says: "For three sins of Israel, even for four, I will not turn back my

wrath. They sell the righteous for silver, and the needy for a pair of sandals. They trample on the heads of the poor as upon the dust of the ground and deny justice to the oppressed. Father and son use the same girl and so profane my holy name. They lie down beside every altar on garments taken in pledge. In the house of their god they drink wine taken as fines."
—Amos 2:6-8 NIV

Hear this, you who trample the needy and do away with the poor of the land, saying, "When will the New Moon be over that we may sell grain, and the Sabbath be ended that we may market wheat?"— skimping the measure, boosting the price and cheating with dishonest scales, buying the poor with silver and the needy for a pair of sandals, selling even the sweepings with the wheat.
—Amos 8:4-6 NIV

People were sometimes sold into slavery for money (silver), and they were sold at other times for property, symbolized by a "pair of sandals." Wealthy people profaned the house of the Lord by drinking wine there after it had been taken as fines from poor people and by lying at the altar on garments of clothing taken as pledges for debts owed. Those debts were unjust and illegal, the result of false judgments and injustices against the poor and needy. Note also in chapter 2, verse 7, that father and son had sexual relations with the same girl, most likely a reference to a household servant. That is just one other way of abusing and taking advantage of a poor and helpless person.

Those in power used force and violence to take the possessions of others who were poor, needy, and powerless. The Bible does not present many details regarding the nature of that violence, but it involved bloodshed, and most likely the taking of people's lives. Two things are clear, however; the shedding of blood was unjustified, and it was widespread.

"Woe to him who builds his palace by unrighteousness, his upper rooms by injustice, making his countrymen work for nothing, not paying them for their labor."...."But your eyes and your heart

are set only on dishonest gain, on shedding innocent blood and on oppression and extortion."
—Jeremiah 22:13,17 NIV

The godly have been swept from the land; not
one upright man remains. All men lie in wait
to shed blood; each hunts his brother with a
net. Both hands are skilled in doing evil; the
ruler demands gifts, the judge accepts bribes,
the powerful dictate what they desire—they all
conspire together.
—Micah 7:2-3 NIV

The word of the Lord came to me: "Son of man,
will you judge her? Will you judge this city of
bloodshed? Then confront her with all her detestable practices...."'See how each of the princes
of Israel who are in you uses his power to shed
blood. In you they have treated father and mother
with contempt; in you they have oppressed the
alien and mistreated the fatherless and widow.'"
—Ezekiel 22:1-2,6-7 NIV

In chapter 22 of the Book of Jeremiah, the prophet proclaims judgment on the evil kings of Judah. Verses 13 and 17 are directed at King Jehoiakim, the son of King Josiah. He acquired his wealth by means of dishonest gain, extortion, cheating of his workers, injustice, oppression of the poor and weak, and shedding of innocent blood. Chapters 6 and 7 of the Book of Micah present a similar charge against Israel. Chapter 7, verses 2 and 3, portray Israel as a land of the ungodly, with the rulers, judges, and people with power taking advantage of the poor and powerless. They too used violence and bloodshed to gain power and wealth. The prophet Ezekiel addressed the sins of the city of Jerusalem, capital of Judah. The people in Jerusalem turned from God to worship idols, and they committed all kinds of detestable sins, including the oppression and mistreatment of aliens, orphans, widows, and other helpless people in their midst. The princes of Israel (the city leaders) were charged with shedding blood to gain power and wealth. Note also in verse 7 that fathers and mothers were not honored in Jerusalem; they were treated with contempt.

The priests in Israel and Judah were responsible for instructing the people in matters of the Law and rendering decisions in areas of conflict. They were to interpret the Mosaic Law and explain it to the people. The priests were as corrupt , however, as the rulers and other people with power.

On the twenty-fourth day of the ninth month, in the second year of Darius, the word of the Lord came to the prophet Haggai: "This is what the Lord Almighty says: 'Ask the priests what the law says:'"....

—Haggai 2:10-11 NIV

"And now this admonition is for you, O priests. If you do not listen, and if you do not set your heart to honor my name," says the Lord Almighty, "I will send a curse upon you, and I will curse your blessings. Yes, I have already cursed them, because you have not set your heart to honor me....."For the lips of the priest ought to preserve knowledge, and from his mouth men should seek instruction—because he is the messenger of the Lord Almighty. But you have turned from the way and by your teaching have caused many to

stumble; you have violated the covenant with Levi," says the Lord Almighty. "So I have caused you to be despised and humiliated before all the people, because you have not followed my ways but have shown partiality in matters of the law."
—Malachi 2:1-2,7-9 NIV

Hear this, you leaders of the house of Jacob, you rulers of the house of Israel, who despise justice and distort all that is right; who build Zion with bloodshed, and Jerusalem with wickedness. Her leaders judge for a bribe, her priests teach for a price, and her prophets tell fortunes for money. Yet they lean upon the Lord and say, "Is not the Lord among us? No disaster will come upon us."
—Micah 3:9-11 NIV

In the Book of Haggai, the prophet was told by the Lord to ask the priest for the meaning, or interpretation, of the Law. The prophet Malachi charged the priests in Judah with shirking their responsibilities. They were guilty of false teaching, causing others to sin, and they had shown partiality in matters of the Law. Those actions brought

God's judgment down on the priests. Chapter 3 of the Book of Micah presents a charge against the rulers, priests, and prophets in Israel and Judah. Included in the despicable practices of the leaders was interpretation of the Law by the priests for a price. If a person suffered a wrong, he or she could go to the priest for a ruling or application of the Law. But, if that person had no money, he or she could not get a hearing before the priest. That was true also for hearings before the corrupt judges and prophets.

We have discussed briefly the divine commands and precepts mediated through Moses to govern the overall conduct of God's people, the Israelites. That Mosaic Law is lengthy and very complex, so it is virtually impossible to obey completely. We have also considered the multitude of sins committed by the Israelites over several centuries. But, the question still unanswered is, "What did the Lord expect of His chosen people, Israel?" Let us review five Scripture passages, which I believe shed some light on that key question.

"I hate, I despise your religious feasts; I cannot stand your assemblies. Even though you bring me burnt offerings and grain offerings, I will not accept them. Though you bring choice fellowship offerings, I will have no regard for them. Away with the noise of your songs! I will not listen to the music of your harps. But let justice roll on like a river, righteousness like a never-failing stream!"

—Amos 5:21-24 NIV

The prophet Amos called for Israel's repentance from their many sins. Through Amos, the Lord rejected the sacrifices and offerings enumerated in the Mosaic Law, and He despised their feasts and other worship assemblies which were also required by the Mosaic Law. God refused to listen to their music and songs, which were supposedly offered up to Him in praise and thanksgiving. Why did God reject the Israelites' offerings, worship rituals, and praise? I believe it was because He considered them all to be insincere; they were just empty words and actions. The people's sinful conduct indicated their worship of God was superficial and insincere.

God does not want halfhearted and insincere worship from His people. Four related Scripture passages tell us what God desires from His people, rather than the legalistic and superficial worship of the Israelites.

And now, O Israel, what does the Lord your God ask of you but to fear the Lord your God, to walk in all his ways, to love him, to serve the Lord your God with all your heart and with all your soul, and to observe the Lord's commands and decrees that I am giving you today for your own good?
—Deuteronomy 10:12-13 NIV

Now all has been heard; here is the conclusion of the matter: Fear God and keep his commandments, for this is the whole duty of man.
—Ecclesiastes 12:13 NIV

And the word of the Lord came again to Zechariah: "This is what the Lord Almighty says: 'Administer true justice; show mercy and compassion to one another. Do not oppress the widow or the fatherless, the alien or the poor. In your hearts do not think evil of each other.'"
—Zechariah 7:8-10 NIV

With what shall I come before the Lord and bow
down before the exalted God? Shall I come before
him with burnt offerings, with calves a year old?
Will the Lord be pleased with thousands of rams,
with ten thousand rivers of oil? Shall I offer my
firstborn for my transgression, the fruit of my
body for the sin of my soul? He has showed you,
O man, what is good. And what does the Lord
require of you? To act justly and to love mercy
and to walk humbly with your God.

—Micah 6:6-8 NIV

The passage in Deuteronomy tells God's chosen people,
and us as well, to reverence the Lord; that is, to recognize who He is, to trust in Him, and to commit to Him.
God's people are also told to walk in His ways and love
Him. That means we are to be obedient to Him in all
we do and put Him first in our lives. We are told also
to serve the Lord with our total being, fully committed
to Him. In the Book of Ecclesiastes, the Teacher (or
Preacher) searched for meaningfulness and fulfillment
in life. He pursued many things in his quest for happi-
ness and satisfaction, including pleasure, power, work,

possessions, and wisdom. But in all of them he found only meaninglessness and emptiness. He ultimately found that a life lived apart from God is not fulfilling, but that a life lived in God's will yields real meaning and true satisfaction. That conclusion is presented in the passage from Ecclesiastes.

The Scripture passage in Zechariah summarizes what the Lord expects from His people with regard to their relationships with others. We should be fair and honest, rendering true judgments, always being kind and compassionate toward others. We are to watch out for and help those in our society who are needy and help-less, and we should not devise evil against one another. The Scripture passage in Micah reflects the real meaning of pure religion. Acceptance by God cannot be achieved by means of offerings and sacrifices or any other reli-gious rituals. Righteous living is the only thing we can do to please the Lord. Our relationship with God cannot be right if we do not have the right relationships with others. We "act justly" by being honest and fair with everyone, by protecting the rights of the weak and help-less people in our midst, and by not showing favoritism toward the rich and powerful in our society. We "love mercy" by fulfilling the obligations in our relationships with others even when we are not required to do so, by loving someone simply because of their need to be loved, and by loving other people sacrificially the way God loved us when He sent His Son to die on a cross for our sins. We can "walk humbly" with God only if we act justly and love mercy in our relationships with one another. Walking humbly with God means reverencing Him, being obedient to Him, obeying His Word, and yielding our will to His perfect will.

I believe the Scripture passages in Micah and Zechariah express the true meaning of pure religion, living our lives as God desires. Note that God asks us to change our attitudes and conduct. But, He does not demand that we change others; that is the Lord's responsibility. We would do well to remember that and apply it in our own lives.

CHAPTER 11

Pure Religion in the New Testament

—ᴟ—

We have defined pure religion as living our lives the way God wants us to. The Old Testament tells us how the Lord dealt with His chosen people, Israel, and what He expected from them. The principles and guidelines for living presented in the Old Testament still applied during New Testament times, and I believe they are relevant to our society in year 2006. The universal Church, which is made up of Christians, or believers, from all time periods, has now become God's people, so I believe the instructions and commands for living included in the New Testament are addressed primarily to the Church and to individual Christians. Let us examine pertinent Scripture passages in the New Testament to determine what God expects from His people today, but we must remember that the principles for living presented in the Old Testament are still applicable in our society.

A major portion of the New Testament is devoted to the birth, life, ministry, teaching, crucifixion, and resurrection of God's Son, and our Savior and Lord, Jesus Christ. The New Testament also speaks extensively about the establishment and growth of the Church in the first century A.D. Presented as well in the New Testament is God's Kingdom, which is with us today in the hearts of believers. Culmination of that Kingdom will occur at the Second Coming of Christ, when all humankind will be relegated to either Heaven or Hell. Those three topics do not relate directly to our discussion of pure religion, so we will not consider them in our study. Another important aspect of Christian living is that of evangelism, the sharing of the Gospel of Jesus Christ, the Good News, with all the people of the world. That sharing of the Good News is demanded of all Christians, thus that aspect of our Christian living is not considered either, but remember that our highest priority should be telling others about Jesus Christ. We spread the Good News by means of our personal witness, the verbal sharing of our faith and the Gospel with others, and by means of our living witness, the way we live our lives. The way we live our lives and how we relate to other people are therefore extremely important.

The question we address now is, "What does God expect of us today, what is pure religion?" The people of Israel lived under the Mosaic Law, a legalistic listing of things they could not do and things they should do. In the Christian era, however, we live under grace rather than under a legalistic set of commandments and precepts, but we do have the Bible as a guideline for our attitudes and conduct. Our goal is to define pure religion from the perspective of the New Testament, but to do so in light of the teaching of the Old Testament. Achieving that goal will enable us to apply the Scriptures to some of the key issues faced by our society today. Hopefully, we can gain a better understanding of the extreme division in America, and perhaps we can identify ways of eliminating some of that partisanship.

Jesus tells us in one of His earliest teachings, the Sermon on the Mount, which is included in the Book of Matthew, chapters 5-7, that He did not come to abolish the Law and the teachings of the prophets, but to fulfill them.

That means the principles presented in the Mosaic Law and the books of the prophets are still relevant today.

> Now when he saw the crowds, he went up on a mountainside and sat down. His disciples came to him, and he began to teach them, saying:....."Do not think that I have come to abolish the Law or the Prophets; I have not come to abolish them but to fulfill them."
> —Matthew 5:1-2,17 NIV

Jesus' Sermon on the Mount informs us that He is more concerned about our attitudes and what is in our hearts than He is about our conduct. Our actions are the result of our internal attitudes, thoughts, biases, priorities, emotions, and motivations. If our heart is truly right, our conduct will be right as well.

> "You have heard that it was said to the people long ago, 'Do not murder, and anyone who murders will be subject to judgment.' But I tell you that anyone who is angry with his brother will be subject to judgment....."You have heard

that it was said, 'Do not commit adultery.' But I tell you that anyone who looks at a woman lustfully has already committed adultery with her in his heart."
—Matthew 5:21-22a,27-28 NIV

"Be careful not to do your 'acts of righteousness' before men, to be seen by them. If you do, you will have no reward from your Father in heaven....."And when you pray, do not be like the hypocrites, for they love to pray standing in the synagogues and on the street corners to be seen by men. I tell you the truth, they have received their reward in full."
—Matthew 6:1,5 NIV

"But the things that come out of the mouth come from the heart, and these make a man 'unclean.' For out of the heart come evil thoughts, murder, adultery, sexual immorality, theft, false testimony, slander. These are what make a man 'unclean';...."
—Matthew 15:18-20a NIV

Jesus is not saying He is unconcerned about the things we say and do. He is simply telling us that our external conduct depends on the condition of our heart, and that if our heart is right, our speech and actions will also be right.

The Apostle Paul admonishes us to live by the indwelling Holy Spirit who is present with all Christians. He speaks of an ongoing internal warfare between our inherently sinful human nature and the indwelling Spirit of God. His teaching about a Spirit-led life is summarized in a Scripture passage from the Book of Galatians.

So I say, live by the Spirit, and you will not gratify the desires of the sinful nature. For the sinful nature desires what is contrary to the Spirit, and the Spirit what is contrary to the sinful nature. They are in conflict with each other, so that you do not do what you want. But if you are led by the Spirit, you are not under law. The acts of the sinful nature are obvious: sexual immorality, impurity and debauchery; idolatry and witchcraft; hatred, discord, jealousy, fits of rage, selfish ambition, dissensions, factions and envy; drunkenness, orgies, and the like. I warn you, as I did before, that those who live like this will not inherit the kingdom of God. But the fruit of the Spirit is love, joy, peace, patience, kindness, goodness, faithfulness, gentleness and self-control. Against such things there is no law. Those who belong to Christ Jesus have crucified the sinful nature with its passions and desires. Since we live by the Spirit, let us keep in step with the Spirit. Let us not become conceited, provoking and envying each other.

—Galatians 5:16-26 NIV

In this passage, Paul presents a contrast between a life controlled by our sinful human nature and a life controlled by the indwelling Holy Spirit. These are referred to as works of the flesh and works of the Spirit, and they involve our physical deeds, our inner attitudes, and our social relationships. Included in works of the flesh are sexual misconduct (sexual immorality, impurity, and debauchery), and sinful religious practices (idolatry and witchcraft). The works of the flesh also involve sinful conflicts and wrong attitudes in our social relationships (hatred, discord, jealousy, fits of rage, selfish ambitions, dissensions, factions, and envy). Disagreements in our social relationships are not necessarily bad, provided they do not lead to dislike and ill feelings toward one another; we should agree to disagree. Paul's works of the flesh include out-of-control and unrestrained pleasure seeking (drunkenness and orgies). Paul ended his list of the works of the flesh with "and the like" to indicate the list is not exhaustive. A life controlled by our evil human nature can lead to all kinds of sinful behavior and wrong attitudes.

In contrast to the works of the flesh, the works of the Spirit (or fruit of the Spirit) lead to a life that is pleasing to God. The fruit of the Spirit are nine inner qualities produced by the Holy Spirit's working in a Christian's life. In essence, it is the character of the Holy Spirit showing forth in the life of a believer. The observing world sees the Spirit of God in the life of an obedient Christian. The nine virtues of the Spirit, namely love, joy, peace, patience, kindness, goodness, faithfulness, gentleness, and self-control, are internalized in a believer. But, those internal attitudes do affect the external behavior of a believer, and they affect his or her relationships with others as well. The challenge for us, therefore, is to live by the Spirit, rather than under the control of our sinful human nature. We have that ongoing spiritual warfare within us between the Spirit and our evil human nature, so we must yield to the Spirit's control of our lives. The more we do that, the more pleasing our lives are to the Lord.

A number of other Scripture passages in the New Testament warn us about sinful activities and attitudes. Some of those sins may seem more grievous to us than others, but we must remember that God hates all sin; sin is sin in God's eyes, and any sin we commit displeases Him. We have a tendency to magnify the sins of others and consider our transgressions to be just "little sins."

> Do you not know that the wicked will not inherit the kingdom of God? Do not be deceived: Neither the sexually immoral nor idolaters nor adulterers nor male prostitutes nor homosexual offenders nor thieves nor the greedy nor drunkards nor slanderers nor swindlers will inherit the kingdom of God.
> —1 Corinthians 6:9-10 NIV

Do not let any unwholesome talk come out of your mouths, but only what is helpful for building others up according to their needs, that it may benefit those who listen. And do not grieve the Holy Spirit of God, with whom you were sealed for the day of redemption. Get rid of all bitterness, rage and anger, brawling and slander, along with every form of malice. Be kind and compassionate to one another, forgiving each other, just as in Christ God forgave you.
—Ephesians 4:29-32 NIV

Finally, all of you, live in harmony with one another; be sympathetic, love as brothers, be compassionate and humble. Do not repay evil with evil or insult with insult, but with blessing, because to this you were called so that you may inherit a blessing.
—1 Peter 3:8-9 NIV

Adulterers, prostitutes, and homosexuals are listed as sinners in the passage from 1 Corinthians. But, are they any more evil than thieves, greedy people, slanderers, and swindlers? What about the wealthy individual who cheats on his or her income taxes and thus steals from our government, and from us? Or, the head of a large corporation who eliminates or reduces employee retirement benefits and therefore swindles the corporation's employees out of promised retirement income? And, what about the individuals, political action committees, and other special-interest groups who spread misrepresentations, innuendos, and untruths about opposition political candidates? Is that not slander? The greedy includes a wide range of sinners; those who covet money and power, those who take advantage of the poor and helpless for personal gain, those who engage in price gouging, those who covet material possessions, and so forth. We must be careful about trying to rank-order sinful activities and behavior.

The passage in the Book of Ephesians focuses on our relationships with other people. The emphasis is on unwholesome speech, that which hurts others, and the internal attitudes expressed in that hurtful speech. Believers are to get rid of such sinful attitudes and replace them with attitudes of kindness, compassion, and forgiveness. We are told in 1 Peter, chapter 3, verses

8-9, to live in harmony with others, and to relate to one another with love, compassion, sympathy, and humbleness. We should not retaliate when we believe we have been wronged in some way; we should forgive those who wronged us instead. Throughout the New Testament, we are told to "put off" all sinful attitudes and behavior and to "put on" virtuous attitudes and conduct, those attributes derived from the fruit of the Spirit.

Let us consider briefly a few other sinful and hurtful attitudes that adversely affect our relationships with others. Favoritism, or partiality, involves preferential treatment of someone because of who they are. Such partiality toward someone can be because of race, nationality, economic class, social status, or other similar factors.

Then Peter began to speak: "I now realize how true it is that God does not show favoritism but accepts men from every nation who fear him and do what is right."

—Acts 10:34-35 NIV

"'Do not pervert justice; do not show partiality to the poor or favoritism to the great, but judge your neighbor fairly.'"

—Leviticus 19:15 NIV

My brothers, as believers in our glorious Lord Jesus Christ, don't show favoritism.....If you really keep the royal law found in Scripture, "Love your neighbor as yourself," you are doing right. But if you show favoritism, you sin and are convicted by the law as lawbreakers. For whoever keeps the whole law and yet stumbles at just one point is guilty of breaking all of it.....Speak and act as those who are going to be judged by the law that gives freedom, because judgment without mercy will be shown to anyone who has not been merciful. Mercy triumphs over judgment!

—James 2:1,8-10,12-13 NIV

The passage in the Book of Acts tells us God is no respecter of persons, that He does not show favoritism toward anyone, and that He accepts any person who reveres Him, regardless of where that person is from and his or her station in life. The passage in the Book of Leviticus instructed the people of Israel, and us as well, to be fair and just to everyone, not showing partiality. That particular passage is included in the Mosaic Law given by the Lord through Moses. James, the half-brother of Jesus, tells us not to show favoritism, and he warns us that if we do show partiality we are sinning by disobeying the Law. He goes on to tell us that disobeying only one point of the Law makes us guilty of breaking the whole Law. The "royal law" referred to by James is the basic law, the source of all other laws pertaining to human relationships. The bottom line is, "Showing favoritism is a sin, and it displeases God."

Self-righteousness is an attitude whereby we consider ourselves to be better than others; we place ourselves on spiritual pedestals. The Pharisees in the New Testament were guilty of being self-righteous, and Jesus came down hard on them because of that attitude of superiority. In essence, we are judging others when we consider them to be spiritually inferior to us.

"Two men went up to the temple to pray, one a Pharisee and the other a tax collector. The

Pharisee stood up and prayed about himself: 'God, I thank you that I am not like other men—robbers, evildoers, adulterers—or even like this tax collector. I fast twice a week and give a tenth of all I get.' "But the tax collector stood at a distance. He would not even look up to heaven, but beat his breast and said, 'God, have mercy on me, a sinner.' "I tell you that this man, rather than the other, went home justified before God. For everyone who exalts himself will be humbled, and he who humbles himself will be exalted."
—Luke 18:10-14 NIV

"Woe to you Pharisees, because you give God a tenth of your mint, rue and all other kinds of garden herbs, but you neglect justice and the love of God. You should have practiced the latter without leaving the former undone. "Woe to you Pharisees, because you love the most important seats in the synagogues and greetings in the marketplaces.
—Luke 11:42-43 NIV

"And when you pray, do not be like the hypocrites, for they love to pray standing in the synagogues and on the street corners to be seen by men. I tell you the truth, they have received their reward in full. But when you pray, go into your room, close the door and pray to your Father, who is unseen. Then your Father, who sees what is done in secret, will reward you."

—Matthew 6:5-6 NIV

"Woe to you, teachers of the law and Pharisees, you hypocrites! You clean the outside of the cup and dish, but inside they are full of greed and self-indulgence. Blind Pharisees! First clean the inside of the cup and dish, and then the outside also will be clean."

—Matthew 23:25-26 NIV

The pious Pharisee in the Book of Luke, chapter 18, considered himself to be spiritually superior to those he classified as sinners, namely the robbers, evildoers, adulterers, and tax collectors. He even boasted about fasting and tithing. On the other hand, the humble tax collector recognized he was a sinner and asked God for mercy. Jesus' response in verse 14 tells us clearly that the Lord is displeased by self-righteousness; He wants us to come before Him humbly and with reverence. Note in the passage in Luke, chapter 11, that Jesus charged the Pharisees with neglecting justice, not being fair and honest with others. Not only does an attitude of self-righteousness affect our relationship with the Lord, it is also damaging in our relationships with other people. The Scripture passages in the Book of Matthew reiterate the teaching in Luke about self-righteousness. The morality and righteousness of the Pharisees were superficial, depending on external rituals and actions that were demanded by the Law. What God really wants from His people are internal virtues derived from His indwelling Spirit, virtues that will be manifested in our sincere love and reverence of Him, together with right relationships with others.

Self-righteousness leads to another sinful attitude, that of judging others. The Bible teaches clearly that only God can judge people, that we should not judge one another. We are not talking about judgments rendered through our judicial system and supported by the laws of our land. We are referring to our judgments of others because they have different value systems, approve of behavior we consider to be sinful, have different religious or political views, or just may be different from us. Numerous Scripture passages deal with judging others, but let us consider just two of them.

> "Do not judge, or you too will be judged. For in the same way you judge others, you will be judged, and with the measure you use, it will be measured to you. "Why do you look at the speck of sawdust in your brother's eye and pay no attention to the plank in your own eye? How can you say to your brother, 'Let me take the speck out of your eye,' when all the time there is a plank in your own eye? You hypocrite, first take the plank out of your own eye, and then you will see clearly to remove the speck from your brother's eye."
> —Matthew 7:1-5 NIV

You, therefore, have no excuse, you who pass judgment on someone else, for at whatever point you judge the other, you are condemning

yourself, because you who pass judgment do the same things. Now we know that God's judgment against those who do such things is based on truth. So when you, a mere man, pass judgment on them and yet do the same things, do you think you will escape God's judgment? Or do you show contempt for the riches of his kindness, tolerance and patience, not realizing that God's kindness leads you toward repentance? But because of your stubbornness and your unrepentant heart, you are storing up wrath against yourself for the day of God's wrath, when his righteous judgment will be revealed. God will "give to each person according to what he has done."
—Romans 2:1-6 NIV

When we judge others, we are in essence attempting to impose our moral beliefs and value systems on them. The passage in Matthew is from Jesus' Sermon on the Mount. He is not referring to a gentle and loving confrontation of someone who is perhaps caught in an obvious sin or wrongdoing. Jesus is talking about self-righteous criticism or condemnation of another person for their actions or conduct. That passage tells us we should not criticize someone else for a small failing while we are harboring a much larger fault in our own lives. We are too often guilty of ignoring or minimizing our own transgressions as we amplify the faults of others. Jesus tells us that when we judge others harshly and without any love, God will judge us with the same severity.

The passage from the Book of Romans has a similar message. In chapter 1 of his letter to the Roman church, the Apostle Paul characterized the sinful and immoral lifestyle of the pagans, or Gentiles, those who had a limited revelation of God. He described the Lord's judgment on the pagan society because of their immorality, their rejection of God, and their arrogance. Then, in chapter 2, Paul confronted the Jews, those who had a much deeper knowledge of God, a greater awareness of sin, and an understanding of God's judgment on sin. The Jews applauded God's judgment of the Gentiles, but they were just as guilty of disobeying the Lord and were practicing the same kind of sins. Paul told the Jews, and he tells us, not to judge others for what we deem to be their faults, because we have the same degree of sin in our lives. Paul has strong words for those who do pass judgment on others. They show contempt for God's kindness, tolerance, and patience, and because of their stubbornness and unrepentant hearts they are storing up wrath against themselves for the day of God's judgment at the end of time. All these and other similar warnings in the Bible make it crystal clear. We should not judge one another; if we do, it is a sin.

There is one other sin all of us are guilty of, the sin of omission. We tend to interpret sin as doing something we are forbidden to do, and we relate righteousness to not doing those forbidden things. However, the Bible tells us that not doing what we know we should do is equally as wrong.

Anyone, then, who knows the good he ought to
do and doesn't do it, sins.
—James 4:17 NIV

Not forgiving someone who has wronged us is a sin. Not showing kindness, compassion, and mercy toward others is a sin. Not helping someone in need is a sin. Not standing up for the weak and helpless in our society is a sin. In essence, not allowing the fruit of the Spirit to be manifested in and through our lives is sinning against God.

Perhaps we are now prepared to define pure religion in light of the teaching of both the Old Testament and the New Testament. The Ten Commandments are the foundation upon which all the provisions of the Mosaic Law are formed. The first four commandments relate to our relationship with God, and the last six relate to our relationships with others. Jesus condensed those Ten Commandments even more in the New Testament.

One of them, an expert in the law, tested him with this question: "Teacher, which is the greatest commandment in the Law?" Jesus replied: "'Love the Lord your God with all your heart and with all your soul and with all your mind.' This is the first and greatest commandment. And the second is like it: 'Love your neighbor as your-self.' All the Law and the Prophets hang on these two commandments."

—Matthew 22:35-40 NIV

One of the teachers of the law came and heard them debating. Noticing that Jesus had given them a good answer, he asked him, "Of all the commandments, which is the most important?" "The most important one," answered Jesus, "is this: 'Hear, O Israel, the Lord our God, the Lord is one. Love the Lord your God with all your heart and with all your soul and with all your mind and with all your strength.' The second is this: 'Love your neighbor as yourself.' There is no commandment greater than these."
—Mark 12:28-31 NIV

First and foremost, God demands that we love, reverence, and obey Him with our entire being. If our relationship with God is not right, we cannot relate to others in the right way. The second commandment is that we love our neighbor. In the context of these Scripture passages, "neighbor" is anyone we come in contact with, both people we like and those we dislike. The "love" we must have for our neighbor is a love that seeks what is best for them, regardless of the cost to us, a sacrificial love exemplified by Jesus Christ when He gave His life on a cross to atone for our sins. All the detailed instructions and precepts in the entire Old Testament hang on those two commandments.

We determined in the previous chapter of this book what God expected from His people, the Israelites, and what He expects from us as well. Passages from the Old Testament Books of Zechariah and Micah summarize what the Lord expects from His people with regard to their relationship with Him and their relationships with others.

And the word of the Lord came again to Zechariah: "This is what the Lord Almighty says: 'Administer true justice; show mercy and compassion to one another. Do not oppress the widow or the fatherless, the alien or the poor. In your hearts do not think evil of each other.'"
—Zechariah 7:8-10 NIV

With what shall I come before the Lord and bow down before the exalted God? Shall I come before him with burnt offerings, with calves a year old? Will the Lord be pleased with thousands of rams, with ten thousand rivers of oil? Shall I offer my firstborn for my transgression, the fruit of my body for the sin of my soul? He has showed you, O man, what is good. And what does the Lord require of you? To act justly and to love mercy and to walk humbly with your God.

—Micah 6:6-8 NIV

God wants us to walk in humble fellowship with Him, reverencing and worshiping Him, being obedient to His Word, and yielding our imperfect will to His perfect will. The Lord desires that His people be fair, honest, and just with everyone. That includes both our personal relationships with others and our standing up for the rights of the poor, weak, and helpless in our society. The Lord also wants us to relate to one another with love, kindness, compassion, and mercy, especially in our treatment of those who cannot help themselves.

One key verse of Scripture in the New Testament sheds additional light on the meaning of pure religion. That verse of Scripture from the Book of James is significant in that it tells us explicitly what is required in pure religion, and implicitly what is not included.

> Religion that God our Father accepts as pure and
> faultless is this: to look after orphans and widows
> in their distress and to keep oneself from being
> polluted by the world.
> —James 1:27 NIV

The pure religion defined by James is a practical religion, a religion carried out through our day-to-day relationships with other people. He tells us how to touch people's lives and how to minister to them in the world in which they live. It involves our willing treatment and care of the poor, needy, and helpless in our society, thus reflecting our concern and compassion for others. Pure religion also involves our own lifestyle, what we say and do. We are to have moral and upright lifestyles, not contaminated by the immorality, corruption, and wickedness in the world around us. Implicit in James' definition of pure religion, I believe, is what it does not include. It does not include our trying to change others. We are not to judge other people, to confront them with a self-righteous attitude, and try to impose our moral beliefs and value systems on them. That means we must be tolerant of other people's religious and moral beliefs and respect their right to be "different" from us. Doing that would eliminate a large part of the division and animosity in our country.

CHAPTER 12

Jesus Christ and the Pharisees

—〜〜—

The Pharisees were a Jewish religious sect who believed in strict adherence to the Mosaic Law. They were considered to be the most religious laymen in the first century A.D. Not only were the Pharisees guardians of the written Law in the Old Testament, they also adhered to numerous oral traditions accumulated and passed down from generation to generation. Those traditions were oral interpretations of the first five books of the Old Testament, and they had been developed and redefined over many generations. The purpose of the oral traditions was to apply the Mosaic Law to all aspects of Jewish life, but they had become extremely complex and burdensome to the Jewish people. Actually, the Pharisees were guilty of using the oral traditions as a means of circumventing the basic requirements of the Law, justifying in their minds disobedience of the Law. The Pharisees maintained spiritual authority with regard to public worship practices, spiritual cleansing, sacrificial offerings, prayer, and various other ritualistic practices. By placing so much emphasis on oral traditions, the Pharisees were essentially teaching human traditions as God's Law.

The Pharisees practiced their own brand of religious fundamentalism, that of trying to impose their interpretations of the Law, in combination with their oral traditions, on the Jewish people, quite often for personal gain. Needless to say, Jesus came down hard on the Pharisees, with 'hypocrites" being His most common characterization of them.

The Pharisees and some of the teachers of the law who had come from Jerusalem gathered around Jesus and saw some of his disciples eating food with hands that were "unclean," that is, unwashed. (The Pharisees and all the Jews do not eat unless they give their hands a ceremonial washing, holding to the tradition of the elders. When they come from the marketplace they do not eat unless they wash. And they observe many other traditions, such as the washing of cups, pitchers and kettles.) So the Pharisees and teachers of the law asked Jesus, "Why don't your disciples live according to the tradition of the elders instead of eating their food with 'unclean' hands?" He replied, "Isaiah was right when he prophesied about you hypocrites; as it is written: "'These people honor me with their lips, but their hearts are far from me. They worship me in vain; their teachings are but rules taught by men.' You have let go of the commands of God and are holding on to the traditions of men." And he said to them: "You have a fine way of setting aside the commands of God in order to observe your own traditions! For Moses said, 'Honor your father and your mother,' and, 'Anyone who curses his father or mother must be put to death.' But you say that if a man says to his father or mother: 'Whatever help you might otherwise have received from me is Corban' (that is, a gift devoted to God), then you no longer let him do anything for his father or mother. Thus you

nullify the word of God by your tradition that you have handed down. And you do many things like that."
—Mark 7:1-13 NIV

Meanwhile, when a crowd of many thousands had gathered, so that they were trampling on one another, Jesus began to speak first to his disciples, saying: "Be on your guard against the yeast of the Pharisees, which is hypocrisy."
—Luke 12:1 NIV

The basic meaning of the word "Pharisees" is separated ones, with the implication being separation from anything unholy or spiritually unclean so they would be fit to serve the Lord. But, the Pharisees had developed an extensive set of detailed instructions pertaining to external cleanliness, or holiness, and they had ignored the need for internal cleansing. They had meticulous rituals and ceremonial laws with regard to hand washing before a meal, cleansing cooking utensils, and cleansing their bodies after touching someone or something "unclean." The traditions of the Pharisees were man-made laws that were in contradiction to the intent of the Mosaic Law.

In the passage from Mark, the Pharisees confronted Jesus about the way His disciples ate with unclean hands. They had not given their hands a ceremonial washing according to the traditions of the Pharisees. The Pharisees were concerned about ritualistic external cleansing rather than the internal condition of the heart; their priority was wrong. Jesus referred to the Pharisees as hypocrites and gave an example of their hypocrisy. The Law demanded that the Israelites honor their fathers and mothers, meaning they must provide them with financial support when needed. But, the Pharisees developed traditions enabling them to circumvent that requirement of the Law. They could declare their financial resources as "Corban," a gift devoted to God, and then they would not be required to use those resources to support their parents. Jesus accused the Pharisees of nullifying God's commands by their many traditions. We see in Luke, chapter 12, verse 1, Jesus warning His disciples about the hypocrisy of the Pharisees.

Another point of contention between the Pharisees and Jesus was how the Sabbath should be observed, an important concern for the Jews. The Pharisees had formulated their own strict requirements for observing the Sabbath. One requirement was that no work could be performed on the Sabbath, and they had made a long and detailed list of what constituted work.

One Sabbath Jesus was going through the grainfields, and his disciples began to pick some heads of grain, rub them in their hands and eat the kernels. Some of the Pharisees asked, "Why are you doing what is unlawful on the Sabbath?" Jesus answered them, "Have you never read what David did when he and his companions were hungry? He entered the house of God, and taking the consecrated bread, he ate what is lawful only for the priests to eat. And he also gave some to his companions." Then Jesus said to them, "The Son of Man is Lord of the Sabbath." On another Sabbath he went into the synagogue and was teaching, and a man was there whose right hand was shriveled. The Pharisees and the teachers of the Law were looking for a reason to accuse Jesus, so they watched him closely to see if he would heal on the Sabbath. But Jesus knew what they were thinking and said to the man with the shriveled hand, "Get up and stand in front of everyone." So he got up and stood there. Then Jesus said to them, "I ask you, which is lawful on the Sabbath: to do good or to do evil, to save life or to destroy it?" He looked around at them all, and then said to the man, "Stretch out your hand." He did so, and his hand was completely restored. But they were furious and began to discuss with one another what they might do to Jesus.

—Luke 6:1-11 NIV

Then he said to them, "The Sabbath was made for man, not man for the Sabbath. So the Son of Man is Lord even of the Sabbath."

—Mark 2:27 NIV

Picking grain was certainly not one of the tasks allowed by the Pharisees on the Sabbath, therefore they confronted Jesus when His disciples began doing so. Jesus reminded the Pharisees of the time in the Old Testament when David and his companions took consecrated bread from the house of God to satisfy their desperate hunger. Eating such consecrated bread was normally considered unlawful, but doing so would be lawful if it was done for good. God established the Sabbath for the good of humankind, to allow people to rest on the seventh day; they would not be required to work on the Sabbath. Jesus' point was that doing good is always in season. The Pharisees even believed it was unlawful to heal someone on the Sabbath if their life was not at risk. Jesus healed the man with the crippled hand to again demonstrate that doing good on the Sabbath was permissible, but the Pharisees were furious because they considered such healing on the Sabbath to be unlawful. Jesus told the Pharisees in the passage from Mark that the Sabbath was established for the good of man, not man for the Sabbath. That is a truth the Pharisees did not comprehend.

Spiritual cleansing and observance of the Sabbath were just two of the numerous points of contention between Jesus and the Pharisees. We find the Pharisees clashing with Jesus throughout the first four books of the New Testament, the four Gospels. Three passages of Scripture indicate the extent of the Pharisees' self-righteousness, arrogance, hypocrisy, selfishness, and animosity toward Jesus.

"Woe to you, teachers of the law and Pharisees, you hypocrites! You give a tenth of your spices— mint, dill and cummin. But you have neglected the more important matters of the law—justice, mercy and faithfulness. You should have prac- ticed the latter, without neglecting the former. You blind guides! You strain out a gnat but swallow a camel. "Woe to you, teachers of the law and Pharisees, you hypocrites! You clean the outside of the cup and dish, but inside they are full of greed and self-indulgence. Blind Pharisees! First clean the inside of the cup and dish, and then the outside also will be clean."
—Matthew 23:23-26 NIV

The Pharisees, who loved money, heard all this and were sneering at Jesus. He said to them, "You are the ones who justify yourselves in the eyes of

men, but God knows your hearts. What is highly valued among men is detestable in God's sight."
—Luke 16:14-15 NIV

When Jesus left there, the Pharisees and the teachers of the law began to oppose him fiercely and to besiege him with questions, waiting to catch him in something he might say.
—Luke 11:53-54 NIV

Jesus criticized the Pharisees for emphasizing the external legalistic provisions of the Law, while neglecting the more important internal matters. The Pharisees had carefully obeyed the Law's requirements for tithing, ritualistic cleansing, public worship practices, observance of the Sabbath, and other such external matters. But, they had ignored the inner qualities demanded by the Law, namely justice, mercy, and faithfulness, among others. Note that Jesus did not condemn the Pharisees for following the Law regarding external matters; He simply admonished them for placing a higher priority in those areas. Jesus wanted the Pharisees, and us, to demonstrate the very important internal attributes in our relationship with God and in our relationships with others. Jesus told the Pharisees in Luke, chapter 16, that they were more concerned about being deemed righteous by other people than they were about being acceptable in God's eyes. The Pharisees continually tried to find ways to discredit Jesus, even to the point of finding justification for putting Him to death. They followed Jesus around waiting to catch Him in something He might say or do.

The Pharisees, the most religious sect of the Jews, were the ones Jesus came down the hardest on in the New Testament. That tells us religious and righteous are not necessarily the same in God's eyes. We must be extremely careful how we view others, not allowing hypocrisy, self-righteousness, arrogance, pride, and selfishness to creep into our attitude toward other people. Instead, we must manifest the fruit of the Spirit, those nine inner virtues, in our relationships with one another. That is the only way we can please God.

CHAPTER 13

Application of Scripture to Today's Society

—⁂—

We discussed at great length the extreme polarization of our country, and we considered some of the major factors contributing to that division. The fundamentalism inherent in the social conservative movement has yielded a religious and moral agenda that, I believe, is a source of much of the bitter division in America. The right-wing ideology and partisan policies of the Republican Party have also contributed significantly to the polarization of our population. The influence of big-money special-interest groups has led to greed and corruption at all levels of our government, along with intense partisanship. The controversial decision by the Bush team to invade Iraq, the lack of planning for the postwar insurgency and reconstruction efforts in Iraq, and the resulting high costs in dollars and American lives have amplified the polarization that already existed. The Bush administration's blatant attempts to increase presidential powers and perpetuate ideological Republican control of our nation have further increased the partisanship in our country.

The Republican Party has embraced the religious and moral agenda of the social conservative movement led by the religious right. Social conservatives have, in turn, accepted the ideological political agenda and policies of the Republican Party. The current Republican Party is essentially defined and characterized by the religious right; social conservatives are in control of the Grand Old Party. This "marriage" of politics and religion has thrust the moral and religious agenda of social conservatives onto center stage in America's political arena. We no longer have separation of church and state in our nation. Our country has a political party, the Republican Party, which: (1) Passionately pursues incorporation of the religious and moral beliefs of the religious right into our nation's laws and government policies, (2) Claims family values as a centerpiece of the party's agenda, (3) Professes to be compassionate conservatives, and (4)

Defines patriots as only those who support President Bush and his unilateral invasion of Iraq. They cast all those issues as struggles between good and evil, and they place the Republican Party on the side of good. They claim God is on their side. But, does the Bible support all the Republican Party's claims?

We turned to the Scriptures, both the Old Testament and the New Testament, to get a clear definition of pure religion, a religion that pleases God. The model for pure religion in the Old Testament is what God demanded from His people, Israel. The Israelite people considered obedience to the legalistic and external provisions of the Mosaic Law to be of utmost importance. That meant following detailed instructions for worship of God, keeping all the feasts and rituals specified in the Law, presenting the required sacrifices and offerings, and keeping all the other precepts pertaining to external conduct and activities. The Bible does not say all those things are bad, but it does say they are of secondary importance to the Lord. What was expected of the Israelites is clearly shown in a passage from the Book of Micah.

With what shall I come before the Lord and bow down before the exalted God? Shall I come before him with burnt offerings, with calves a year old? Will the Lord be pleased with thousands of rams, with ten thousand rivers of oil? Shall I offer my firstborn for my transgression, the fruit of my body for the sin of my soul? He has showed you, O man, what is good. And what does the Lord require of you? To act justly and to love mercy and to walk humbly with your God.

—Micah 6:6-8 NIV

What God expected from the Israelites was a lifestyle based on inner attitudes and virtues, rather than a lifestyle characterized by legalized deeds and actions. God required the people of Israel to reverence Him and obey His commands, to be fair and just with everyone, and to love others with a sacrificial love that seeks what is best for them. God asked the Israelites to change their own attitudes and conduct, but He did not ask them to change the attitudes and behavior of others. That basic definition of pure religion is in evidence throughout the Old Testament. God demands that His people be just, honest, and compassionate toward everyone, but especially toward the poor and powerless in their midst.

The New Testament presents a similar definition of pure religion, what the Lord desires from His people, the Church. Jesus condensed the entire teaching of the Old Testament into two basic commandments; to love God, and to love others. Jesus is more concerned about the condition of our hearts than He is about our external actions. He taught that if our hearts are right, then our behavior will also be right. Our external deeds, what we say and do, are the result of our inner attitudes, priorities, thoughts, desires, and biases. The Apostle Paul emphasized a Spirit-led life, a life controlled by the indwelling Holy Spirit, as opposed to a life under the control of our evil human nature. The indwelling Spirit produces nine inner qualities in the life of a Christian, referred to by Paul as the fruit of the Spirit. Those nine inner qualities, or virtues, affect the external behavior of a believer, as well as his or her relationships with others. The more we allow the Spirit to control our lives, the more pleasing we are to God.

The teaching of Jesus in the New Testament does not abolish the Mosaic Law and the teaching of the prophets in the Old Testament; Jesus said He came to fulfill the Law and the Prophets. That means the principles for living presented in the Old Testament are still relevant today. One verse of Scripture in the Book of James sums up the New Testament definition of pure religion.

Religion that God our Father accepts as pure and faultless is this: to look after orphans and widows in their distress and to keep oneself from being polluted by the world.

—James 1:27 NIV

We love because he first loved us. If anyone says, "I love God," yet hates his brother, he is a liar. For anyone who does not love his brother, whom he has seen, cannot love God, whom he has not seen. And he has given us this command: Whoever loves God must also love his brother.

—1 John 4:19-21 NIV

James, the half-brother of Jesus, defines pure religion in much the same way as the prophet Micah in the Old Testament. James does not specifically mention our worship and reverence of God, but the New Testament teaches clearly that we cannot have a right relationship with others if we do not have a right relationship with the Lord. Verses 19-21 of 1 John, chapter 4, emphasize that truth. James does tell us we are to have moral and upright lifestyles, not contaminated by the immorality, corruption, and wickedness in the world around us. Pure religion, as defined by James, also involves our willing care of and assistance to the poor, needy, and helpless in our society, thus reflecting our concern and compassion for others. Neither James' definition of pure religion in the New Testament nor Micah's definition of pure religion in the Old Testament includes our trying to change the attitudes and conduct of others. That is an important Biblical truth we must remember.

James' view of pure religion is evident throughout the New Testament. The Scriptures tell us repeatedly to worship God, to reverence Him, and to obey Him. We are told over and over in the Bible to put off immorality, wickedness, and all forms of evil in our own lives. The Bible also demands that we relate to others with love, mercy, justice, compassion, and kindness, allowing the fruit of the Spirit to shine forth in our relationships with one another. The Bible does not instruct us to confront others with what we perceive to be their sinful behavior, and neither does it tell us to try and change the attitudes and behavior of other people. Actually, the Scriptures teach us just the opposite.

"Do not judge, or you too will be judged. For in the same way you judge others, you will be judged, and with the measure you use, it will be measured to you. "Why do you look at the speck of sawdust in your brother's eye and pay no attention to the plank in your own eye? How can you say to your brother, 'Let me take the speck out of your eye,' when all the time there is a plank in your own eye? You hypocrite, first take the plank out of your own eye, and then you will see clearly to remove the speck from your brother's eye."
—Matthew 7:1-5 NIV

The Bible instructs us not to criticize and judge one another because we have the same degree of sin in our own lives. The Scriptures tell us plainly to always relate to one another with mercy, kindness, compassion, forgiveness, and love, rather than with self-righteousness, arrogance, haughtiness, criticism, slander, malice, and judgment. The Bible informs us what to do and what not to do, but it does not instruct us to tell others what they should do and should not do. Judgment belongs exclusively with God, and we should never try to usurp God's authority.

So, how does the New Testament teaching on pure religion apply to the religious and moral issues of today's society? The religious right, and for the most part the Republican Party, are passionate, outspoken, and active in opposing abortion, euthanasia, homosexuality, and gay marriage. The intent of this study is not to either affirm their beliefs about those controversial issues or to refute them. Let us look instead at the manner in which social conservatives pursue those hot-button issues, and the way they relate to people on opposite sides of the issues. What do they say about, and how do they treat, doctors and medical clinics that counsel young women contemplating abortion and also doctors who perform abortions? Or, what is the religious right's attitude toward doctors who counsel and assist terminally ill and suffering patients regarding euthanasia? Do the religious right and right-wing Republicans relate to those doctors and clinic personnel with the attributes of the Holy Spirit, or do they relate to them with self-righteousness, contempt, arrogance, sometimes even hate, and judgment? When Pro-Life proponents block entrances to abortion clinics and harass young women entering those clinics, what kind of attitude are they displaying? Is it one of love, kindness, and compassion, or is it an attitude of self-righteousness, derision, malice, and judgment? I believe we know the answers to those questions.

And, what is the attitude and behavior of social conservatives toward homosexuals in general, and gay couples in particular, the products of either civil unions or gay marriages? Is the fruit of the Spirit manifested in their relationships with homosexuals, or do they relate to them with derision, scorn, even acts of violence, self-righteousness, and judgment? We must keep in mind, however, that the abortion, euthanasia, homosexuality, and gay marriage issues are double-sided coins. We find some of God's people on both sides of all those issues. Regardless of our beliefs about the individual issues,

AMERICA, A HOUSE DIVIDED

we should not relate to people on the opposing sides with self-righteousness, any kind of malice, or judgment. Our attitudes and actions should evolve from the internal virtues of the Holy Spirit produced in the lives of Christians. That is the only way we can please God. May each of us examine our own heart and determine if our attitudes and actions on those controversial issues are what God expects from us.

Social conservatives are passionate about other issues as well. They push for school-sponsored Christian prayer in our public schools, they strive to display the Ten Commandments in government facilities, and they demand that creationism be taught in our public schools' science classes. They are essentially working to tear down the wall of separation between church and state, a wall inherent in our Constitution and Bill of Rights, and a policy that has served our nation well for over two hundred years. The basic goal of the religious right is to impose their Christian religious beliefs and practices on everyone in our country, Christian and non-Christian alike. The above three issues, prayer in public schools, display of the Ten Commandments, and teaching of creationism in our public schools, are all legalistic external matters, somewhat analogous to the rituals and other legalistic practices of the people of Israel in the Old Testament. What God really desires from His people, the Church, are internal attitudes and internal attributes produced by the indwelling Holy Spirit, resulting in right behavior and right relationships with one another. It seems to me social conservatives have focused on legalistic external matters that are actually in violation of our nation's Constitution and Bill of Rights, and they have neglected those internal matters desired by the Lord. Is that not what the rebellious Israelites did in the Old Testament, leading to God's judgment on the nations of Israel and Judah?

The Republican Party, with the loyal support of social conservatives, has consistently passed legislation and regulations that benefit our wealthier citizens and large corporations. At the same time, they have steadily reduced funding for programs that help the poor, needy, and helpless in our society. How can the religious right and Republicans justify such action? They maintain it is not the government's responsibility to take care of people, that such responsibility belongs to their families and churches. They argue also that the Bible does not instruct the government to take care of people, that such instructions in the Old Testament are not relevant to today's society. Republicans claim the prophets' commands to the rulers and leaders of the Israelites to help the poor and helpless were addressed only to Israel, and not to our government today. Are their claims true?

The same social conservatives and Republicans who argue that the Old Testament is not relevant today with regard to justice, mercy, and care for the powerless turn to somewhat vague Scripture passages in the Old Testament Book of Psalms to justify their rigid stance on abortion. And, they turn to Old Testament passages to support their stand on homosexuality. Furthermore, social conservatives and a majority of Republicans want to display the Ten Commandments, an Old Testament passage, in government buildings, and they push for teaching of Old Testament creationism in our public schools. Social conservatives seem to pick and choose Old Testament passages that they interpret to be justification for their positions on controversial issues, but they choose to ignore other Old Testament passages, claiming they are irrelevant in today's society. They want to have it both ways. Jesus Himself tells us He did not come to abolish the Law and the Prophets , meaning the entire Old Testament. He came to fulfill them instead.

> "Do not think that I have come to abolish the Law or the Prophets; I have not come to abolish them but to fulfill them."
> —Matthew 5:17 NIV

That one verse of Scripture tells me the principles of living presented in the Old Testament are still relevant today. Included are the prophets' commands to the rulers, judges, religious leaders, and wealthy people to care for, provide for, and stand up for the poor, needy, and helpless in their midst. The religious right and many Republicans claim the Bible as their guide for living, including imposing their religious beliefs and moral values on all our citizens, but they seem to ignore portions of the Bible that are in conflict with their views. Could that be hypocrisy?

Social conservatives also argue the Bible does not say the government is responsible for helping the poor and powerless in our society. They maintain that all Scripture passages pertaining to such help are directed to individuals and the Church, rather than to the government. It is my view that the New Testament passages do not specifically rule out help from the government. When the Bible commands us to "look out" for the powerless in our midst, I believe those instructions are directed to everyone, including individuals, families, churches, local governments, state governments, and the federal government. If the New Testament writers meant to exclude the government from that responsibility, I believe they would have said so.

The Bible speaks out against greed and corruption, and it condemns worship of any thing or anyone other than God. We do not worship idols, images, and other pagan deities in our society, but are there other things we do worship instead? Any thing we place above the Lord in our priorities is the object of our worship. When we put pursuit of wealth, our careers, our hobbies, social standing, political power, education, pleasure, or any other thing first in our life, we are worshiping that thing. Jesus sums it up nicely.

"No one can serve two masters. Either he will hate the one and love the other, or he will be

devoted to the one and despise the other. You cannot serve both God and Money."
—Matthew 6:24 NIV

A culture of greed, corruption, and power grabbing is evident throughout our society, especially in our federal and state governments. We discussed the greed and corruption associated with: Special-interest lobbying activities in Washington; The disastrous results of a Republican administration and a Republican-controlled Congress beholden to wealthy people and large corporations; The fraud and corruption rampant in the Iraq reconstruction work; The price-gouging, fraud, and overall corruption in the Department of Homeland Security handling of the Hurricane Katrina disaster; The sacrifice of clean air, clean water, and unpolluted land on the altar of corporate profits; Manipulation and control of our news media by the Bush administration; and Blatant power grabbing by the Bush administration. Is all that greed and corruption in America a manifestation of the Holy Spirit's working in the lives of God's people, or is it the product of lives controlled by our evil and depraved human nature? I do not believe such behavior pleases God, so the Holy Spirit is not in control in our country.

Social conservatives and Republicans claim to be compassionate conservatives, and they profess to be the family-values political party. Yet they fail to provide for, and stand up for, the powerless in our society, and their political agenda and policies favor the well-heeled people and large corporations. That is what the Bible refers to as partiality, and it is a sin; favoritism displeases God. I see scant compassion for the poor in the Republican political agenda, so perhaps their brand of family values is only for the wealthy and well-connected families. Their policies certainly do not strengthen poor and needy families, which to me is what family values is all about. The best way to help and strengthen poor families is to provide a quality education for everyone, make adequate health care accessible to all of our citizens, ensure all workers can earn livable wages, provide affordable housing for the working poor, and provide poor people with whatever financial assistance is necessary. That would be a genuine family-values political agenda, not just a political slogan.

How does the Bible relate to the negative politics, mud slinging, and character assassination championed by the religious right and the Republican Party? They flood the media with misrepresentations, innuendos, and outright lies about opposition candidates. That is true for wealthy individuals, political action committees, candidates' campaigns, special-interest groups, and the Republican Party. But, those identities are all controlled by individuals who make the decisions to put out such garbage against their opponents. The Bible addresses that issue head-on throughout the New Testament.

Do not let any unwholesome talk come out of your mouths, but only what is helpful for building others up according to their needs, that it may benefit those who listen. And do not grieve the Holy Spirit of God, with whom you were sealed for the day of redemption. Get rid of all bitterness, rage and anger, brawling and slander, along with every form of malice. Be kind and compassionate to one another, forgiving each other, just as in Christ God forgave you.

—Ephesians 4:29-32 NIV

Finally, all of you, live in harmony with one another; be sympathetic, love as brothers, be compassionate and humble. Do not repay evil with evil or insult with insult, but with blessing, because to this you were called so that you may inherit a blessing.
— 1 Peter 3:8-9 NIV

Personal attacks and character assassination are not the same as criticism of opposing candidates' stands on the issues and criticism of political parties' policies and initiatives. Political ads should be limited to debates about the issues. The Bible does not tell us to always agree with one another, never to have differences of opinion. It does instruct us, however, to live in harmony, with mutual respect and compassion for one another. Malice toward others, lying, slander, and other such attitudes and actions are condemned in Scripture; they are sins, and all sin displeases God.

What does the Bible say about patriotism? The Republican Party and social conservatives seem to define patriotism as supporting President Bush and his invasion of Iraq. Right-wing zealots brand those opposed to the president and his war in Iraq as unpatriotic, and they have used that definition of patriotism to slander and discredit opposition candidates. To me, standing up for what is best for our country is true patriotism. That could involve fighting in a war against an enemy who has attacked our country, or it could be standing up for the rights of our powerless citizens. Patriotism is not shelling out huge tax subsidies and tax cuts to the wealthy and big business, to the detriment of everyone else. Neither is it awarding lucrative no-bid contracts to political cronies and the well connected, nor is it allowing major financial supporters to pollute our air, water, and land for financial gain. Wrapping one's self in the flag and claiming to be patriotic does not make a patriot. Doing what is best for our country, regardless of cost to self , does indeed make a true patriot. Slandering someone with a phony definition of patriotism is a sin, and it displeases God.

We have discussed the attitudes and actions of the religious right, social conservatives, and the Republican Party, but we have said very little about liberals, moderate conservatives, and the Democratic Party. Does that mean the Democratic Party and its supporters are not guilty of having wrong attitudes and sinful behavior? No, the Democratic Party is guilty of the same kinds of wrongdoings that have characterized the Republican Party, but not to the same extent. Most Democrats are not as passionate, and not as outspoken, about the issues, especially those hot-button religious and moral issues. And, they are certainly not as well connected with regard to big-money interests and special-interest lobbyists. As a result, the Democratic Party does not face the same degree of pressure from special-interest lobbyists to hand out favors to large financial contributors. Democrats are more sensitive to environmental concerns, so they are inherently against the absurd corporate handouts to companies that pollute our air, water, and land. Another huge factor is control of the White House and Congress. The Republicans are in firm control of the Executive and Legislative Branches of our government, thus the Democratic Party has little opportunity to dictate the political agenda. Last but not least, the Democratic Party is champion of the poor and working class, therefore they are not guilty of favoring our wealthiest citizens and large corporations over the lower and middle classes of our population.

The Bible addresses many other issues in our society, but I believe we have touched on those key issues that have caused a majority of the division in America. Each one of us should carefully assess our own position on all the issues and determine if we must make any changes in our attitudes and conduct regarding those issues. May we allow the indwelling Holy Spirit to guide us in our actions and in our relationships with other people. Doing that, I believe, would eliminate much of the animosity and polarization in our country.

CHAPTER 14

How Can Our Country Be United Again?

—ᴍ—

The extreme polarization of America is evident throughout our society, and it touches every segment of our population. We see bitterness, animosity, and strife at all levels of our government, across the political spectrum of our country, throughout the diverse religious realm of our nation, across racial and ethnic segments of our citizenry, in all social and economic classes of our people, and in our various news media. We identified and discussed a number of factors leading to the sharp division in our country, most of which are closely related. We reviewed numerous Scripture passages in both the Old Testament and the New Testament to determine what God expects from His people. We then applied those Bible passages to the major areas of conflict in our society, attempting to identify those attitudes and actions of our people that displease God.

The big question now is, "What must America do to reduce the partisanship in our population, to bring our nation back together?" All of our people do not have to agree on the issues, but we all must strive for the common good of our country as a whole. That means each of us must sacrifice and compromise in some way to build a society which is fair and just to everyone, and one which demonstrates concern and compassion for the powerless in our nation as well as those in countries around the world. It is imperative, I believe, that we succeed in doing that if America hopes to maintain its status as the world's greatest military, economic, and political power, and if it is to gain back the respect and admiration of people around the world.

> Jesus knew their thoughts and said to them, "Every kingdom divided against itself will be ruined, and every city or household divided against itself will not stand."
> —Matthew 12:25 NIV

I sincerely believe this verse of Scripture applies to the United States of America in year 2006. World history provides a record of the many world powers that have collapsed because of internal strife, corruption, economic chaos, and lack of compassion for its weaker subjects. One of the most recent and most notable examples is the Soviet Union collapse some twenty years ago.

There is no easy and sure way to roll back the extreme polarization developed in America over the last twenty-five years or so. The sharp division developed one issue at a time, and I believe it must be eliminated one issue at a time. I do not claim to have a magic cure for our divided country, but let us consider possible areas in which the partisanship could be reduced. In one way or another, all of our nation's polarization involves politics, the sharp disagreements between the Republican Party and the Democratic Party. So, any solution must also involve politics, a joint effort between Republicans and Democrats. In other words, both sides must compromise to some extent and work together on the issues to achieve common good for our country. That is a tall order considering the degree of animosity and strife between the two parties.

The corrupting influence of big money and special-interest groups on our political system is obvious. Wealthy individuals, large corporations, political action committees, and a myriad of special-interest groups contribute the big bucks necessary to get their candidates elected. Those elected officials are then beholden to their large contributors, and are thus compelled to enact laws and regulations favorable to their supporters if they hope to survive the next election cycle. Big money is in control of our political system. Wealthy contributors fund a majority of the slanderous, untruthful, and misleading television political ads that are the source of a significant portion of the animosity and division in our country. Powerful and corrupt lobbyists have access to a lot of the big bucks contributed by wealthy individuals and special-interest groups. The lobbyists use those large sums of money to pressure, coerce, and bribe government officials, who then pass laws and regulations that benefit the lobbyists' clients. A prime example of such a corrupt lobbyist is Jack Abramoff, who has pleaded guilty to bribery and corruption charges. Somehow, this flow of corruptive cash to our politicians must be stopped. It is imperative that Congress unites, including both Republicans and Democrats, to enact bipartisan legislation to drastically limit and control political contributions. If our elected officials refuse to do so, the citizens of our nation must make their voices heard and vote them out of office. The people of America must reclaim control of our country from big-money interests. That is what democracy is all about.

Asking Congress to unite on almost any issue is expecting a lot considering today's political climate in Washington, but I believe the future of our country depends on a truly bipartisan Congress. That does not mean Republicans and Democrats have to agree on all the issues. There will always be differences of opinion on key issues, and partisan debates will certainly take place as legislation moves through the House of Representatives and the Senate. But, both sides must be willing to compromise and seek a meeting-of-the-minds on crucial matters. Both Republicans and Democrats must strive to do what is best for our entire population, and not necessarily what is advantageous for their own political party and their individual constituencies. It is only in such a bipartisan environment in Washington that we will again see true statesmen surface in the halls of Congress.

In order to achieve a bipartisan spirit in Congress, I believe two things must happen. First, the leadership and control of both houses of Congress must be equally divided between Republicans and Democrats, regardless of which party enjoys a majority. The days of secret agreements behind closed doors, shutting the minority party out of all decisions, and using other heavy-handed tactics to run over the opposition must come to an end. Voters, we are the ones who can force that to happen. Second, and most important, members of Congress must change their attitudes and actions toward one another. Senators and representatives must develop a mutual respect for their peers, regardless of the differences in opinion they may have on the issues or which political party they represent. They must refrain from ugly personal attacks on opposing members and stop trying to cast all the issues as good versus evil. Members of Congress should debate the issues, seek compromises that are beneficial for our country, and vote their consciences on the final versions of legislation. And, they should do so without exhibiting the partiality, self-righteousness, arrogance, and judgmental attitude we see in Congress today. Let the fruit of the Spirit be evident in our politicians' relationships with one another.

Achieving a truly bipartisan Congress would be a giant step forward in reducing the polarization of our population, but Congress must do more. We have an Executive Branch of government out of control, with virtually no oversight by Congress. Congress must take steps to rein in the Bush administration, roll back the power-grabbing of the Executive Branch over the last six years, stop the blatant illegal activities of the Bush team, curtail the use of signing statements by the president to circumvent the intent of laws passed by Congress, and establish an effective and ongoing means of congressional oversight of the Executive Branch. Many of our current problems and the extreme polarization of our citizens are a direct result of the Bush administration's usurping of power, including starting an unjustified war with Iraq, rollback of critical environmental regulations, the massive fraud and corruption scandal associated with the reconstruction efforts in Iraq, bungling of the Hurricane Katrina disaster response along with the fraud and corruption rampant in the relief and reconstruction efforts in its aftermath, illegal long-term imprisonment and torture of prisoners in Abu Ghraib and similar secret prisons around the world, and illegal wiretapping of American citizens. Such blatant power-grabbing must be stopped if our nation has any hopes of eliminating the bitter division we see today.

We discussed in chapter 5 of this book the shortcomings of the Department of Homeland Security, made evident by the lack of timely and effective government response after Hurricane Katrina. The Department of Homeland Security is a huge and unwieldy government bureaucracy that has been staffed largely by political cronies of the Bush administration, rather than by qualified people with experience in intelligence work or emergency management. In addition, a Republican Congress has used much of the homeland security funding to reward Congressmen and Congresswomen who support the Republican Party's positions on key issues. Earmarks, or pork-barrel funding, have been used to direct homeland security funds to congressional district projects not related to homeland security. That is political payback. Very little control exists with regard to expenditures within the Department of Homeland

Security. Award of lucrative no-bid contracts to favored contractors is the norm in the department, and a large portion of the homeland security funding is wasted through fraud and corruption, especially in disaster relief and reconstruction efforts similar to those in the aftermath of Hurricane Katrina.

In my opinion, two significant changes are needed in the Department of Homeland Security. The first is to separate FEMA from the department, including separate funding for FEMA and staffing it with key people possessing extensive experience in emergency management. Preparation for, and response to, natural disasters are appreciably different from that of combating terrorism, so those two tasks should be separated. Keep in mind, though, that close coordination and cooperation between FEMA and the Department of Homeland Security is a necessity. The second change is more drastic, because the Department of Homeland Security and FEMA must be bipartisan. That means key positions should be filled with equal numbers of Republicans and Democrats, and all nominees to those key positions should be selected and approved by a bipartisan congressional committee, with White House input. Such a process would tend to eliminate the current politicizing of the Department of Homeland Security. In addition, a bipartisan oversight committee (which could be the same committee) having equal numbers of Republicans and Democrats must have the authority to ensure efficient and timely performance of homeland security and FEMA operations. That oversight committee must have the responsibility to ascertain that adequate planning and preparation for emergencies are in place, and that communication, cooperation, and coordination are maintained between FEMA and the Department of Homeland Security. The congressional oversight committee must also take whatever steps necessary to root out fraud and corruption.

The war in Iraq has proven to be a huge point of contention in our country. In chapter 4 herein, we discussed the merits of the unilateral invasion of Iraq, the severe lack of planning for the strong insurgency after the initial phase of the war, and the bungling of the overall operation by the Bush administration. Nonetheless, our troops are there now, and tremendous problems must be resolved before our military can start to withdraw our soldiers. Iraq is now a breeding ground for terrorism, what we do in Iraq affects our relations with the entire Arab world, and our country desperately needs the oil supplied by the Arab nations in the Middle East. The cost paid with American lives has been high, the financial burden on our nation is great, and our people have lost faith in the leadership of our country. So, where do we go from here?

It is imperative, I believe, that President Bush admit his many mistakes regarding Iraq and replace the inner circle of advisors who led him down the wrong path. He must clean house, replacing his Vice President, Secretary of Defense, Secretary of State, and all the other civilian and military advisors who contributed to the Iraq fiasco. They must be replaced with a group of bipartisan civilian and military officials who have extensive experience in military matters and the Arab culture as well. This group of advisors must be made up of both Republicans and Democrats, and they must be individuals who are not afraid to tell the president something he does not want to hear. I believe such a group of experts could develop a plan to do only what is absolutely necessary in Iraq and then bring our troops home in a timely manner. America made the mess in Iraq, and America should clean it up before we pull out; we owe that to the people of Iraq. It is highly unlikely President Bush will back off from his present position on Iraq, so perhaps Congress should force his hand, even going as far as impeachment if necessary.

The Bush administration has manipulated and coerced the news media to limit and control information released to citizens of our country. Our various news media perform vital and necessary functions in our society, and we must have a free press, one that is not under government control. I admire and respect journalists and reporters who risk their lives to keep us informed about the status of the war in Iraq, major disasters in progress, and other trouble spots around the world. In today's political environment, many of them put their careers on the line to keep us informed about corruption and wrongdoing in our local, state, and federal governments. We have to rely on the news media to be the watchdog over industry and government agencies. So, it behooves Congress to enact legislation and provide oversight so we can maintain what is truly a free and unbiased news media. That will help reduce the bitter division in our country.

Our nation's tax policies are unfair and unjust, heavily tilted toward wealthy people and large corporations. Much of that bias favoring the rich is due to the significant influence of big money in American politics. Rich folks and big business contribute the big bucks necessary to get candidates elected, and the elected officials, in turn, reward their large financial backers with generous tax cuts and tax subsidies. Poor people and the middle class are thus left out in the cold; they have to carry an unequal share of the tax burden. Another factor that adds to the problem is the inherent ideology of the Republican Party. Republicans do not like taxes of any kind, especially those on the wealthy, and they have implemented tax policies that emphasize tax cuts directed primarily at wealthy people and large corporations. Such an unfair tax policy obviously results in animosity and division between the have's and the have-not's. Having a truly bipartisan Congress, one that strives for compromise and fairness, will go a long way toward correcting our current tax inequalities.

Our enormous federal debt, caused by large budget deficits, threatens America's economic future. Our national debt will surpass eight trillion dollars by the end of year 2006, up substantially from what it was when George Bush became president less than six years ago. That obscene debt has not resulted directly in much polarization of our country, but a day of reckoning looms in our future. For the most part, average Americans are not overly concerned about our huge national debt because it has not affected their way of life that much. We were not asked to sacrifice and pay as we go as the Bush administration spent hundreds of billions of dollars in Iraq, gave hundreds of billions to the rich in the form of tax cuts and tax subsidies, implemented other massive corporate giveaways, allocated billions in pork-barrel spending, gave billions to insurance and pharmaceutical companies as part of the Medicare prescription drug program, and spent hundreds of billions on an ineffective and corrupt Department of Homeland Security. Our nation has not experienced a lot of polarization because of the budget deficits themselves, because they have not caused a lot of hardships on our citizens; Americans are living high on borrowed money. But, the factors leading to the large budget deficits have caused sharp disagreements and division. A bipartisan Congress must take drastic action to eliminate the budget deficits and start paying down the national debt. President Clinton and his administration proved it can be done while maintaining a healthy economy. Inaction will lead to economic disaster for America, so our citizens must prepare to make economic sacrifices in the not-distant future.

The social conservative movement has spawned widespread animosity and division over moral and social issues. The religious right has strong and inflexible beliefs about hot-button issues such as abortion and gay marriage, and they strive diligently to incorporate their religious beliefs and practices into our nation's laws and government policies. Social conservatives have essentially taken over the Republican Party, and their fundamentalist agenda is part of the Republican Party platform. The Grand Old Party has always stood for small government, but the Bush administration has grown a huge bloated bureaucracy. Republicans have always championed balanced federal budgets as well, but they are now responsible for the largest budget deficits in our nation's history. Also, Republicans claim to believe in states' rights and local control of our schools, but they pass unfunded mandates down to state schools, and Republican federal judges overturn state court decisions. Republicans have historically stood up for citizens' rights, but now they want the federal government in our bedrooms. Mainstream fiscal conservatives must seize back control of their party from the religious right and radical right-wing ideologists. Perhaps then, a truly bipartisan Congress will be possible, and much of the partisanship over religious and moral issues can be reduced.

The sharp division in our country has been primarily between the extreme right-wing elements of the Republican Party and the extreme left-wing segment of the Democratic Party. I am convinced a large majority of our citizens are either mainstream Republicans, mainstream Democrats, or middle-of-the-road independents, but they have allowed the fringe elements of the two parties to set the political agenda. Mainstream America must get more involved in our political process and take back control of our country. That would go a long way toward eliminating the extreme polarization of our citizenry.

Finally, a great deal of the sharp division in America can be traced back to individual citizens like you and me;

our attitudes and our actions are not what they should be. The Bible tells us to let our lives reflect the fruit of the Spirit, those nine virtues produced in a believer through the internal work of the indwelling Holy Spirit. The alternative is to let our lives be controlled by our evil human nature. Control of our lives by our evil human nature leads to attitudes of greed, selfishness, discord, jealousy, favoritism, self-righteousness, judgmental thinking, and all kinds of malice. These negative internal attributes result in problems in our relationships with others. Such lives controlled by our evil human natures are, I believe, the basic source of the animosity and division in our country.

On the other hand, lives that reflect the fruit of the Spirit, namely love, joy, peace, patience, kindness, goodness, faithfulness, gentleness, and self-control, lead to right relationships with others, thus eliminating animosity and division. That should challenge all of us to examine our hearts and make whatever changes necessary in our own lives. May each of us do our part in reducing the extreme partisanship in our nation, and may God bless our United States of America.

—◊—

Also by Herschel Hill

Looking Toward Eternity: A Life Hereafter?

—ᘻ—

To order additional copies of

AMERICA, A HOUSE DIVIDED

Have your credit card ready and call:
1-866-~~384~~-BOOK (2665)
909

Or visit our web site at:

www.xulonpress.com

Also available at:

www.amazon.com

www.barnesandnoble.com

www.target.com

www.borders.com

and

Through Bookstores

Printed in the United States
57845LVS00004B/103-510

9 781600 344367